OPEN
TO
WORK

HOW TO GET AHEAD IN THE AGE OF AI

OPEN TO WORK

RYAN ROSLANSKY
Chief Executive Officer, LinkedIn
& ANEESH RAMAN
Chief Economic Opportunity Officer, LinkedIn

HarperCollins*Publishers*

HarperCollins*Publishers*
1 London Bridge Street
London SE1 9GF

www.harpercollins.co.uk

HarperCollins*Publishers*
Macken House, 39/40 Mayor Street Upper
Dublin 1, D01 C9W8, Ireland

First published by HarperCollins*Publishers* 2026

1 3 5 7 9 10 8 6 4 2

© LinkedIn Corporation 2026

Ryan Roslansky and Aneesh Raman assert the moral
right to be identified as the authors of this work

A catalogue record of this book is
available from the British Library

HB ISBN 978-0-00-877065-5
PB ISBN 978-0-00-877066-2

Printed and bound in the UK using 100%
renewable electricity at CPI Group (UK) Ltd

All rights reserved. No part of this publication may be
reproduced, stored in a retrieval system, or transmitted,
in any form or by any means, electronic, mechanical,
photocopying, recording or otherwise, without the
prior written permission of the publishers.

Without limiting the exclusive rights of any author, contributor
or the publisher of this publication, any unauthorised use of
this publication to train generative artificial intelligence (AI)
technologies is expressly prohibited. HarperCollins also exercise
their rights under Article 4(3) of the Digital Single Market
Directive 2019/790 and expressly reserve this publication
from the text and data mining exception.

Our vision at LinkedIn is to create economic opportunity for every member of the global workforce. This book is dedicated to every member. To you, in fact. No matter where you live or what you do, no matter what kind of job title you hold or what kind of career trajectory you're on, this book is for you, about you, and how nothing, not even AI, can beat you at being you.

Contents

Foreword 1
Preface 7
Introduction: Failure Is Not an Option 11

PART I: THE WAKE-UP CALL
CHAPTER 1: Buckle Up 27
CHAPTER 2: Let It Go 47
CHAPTER 3: The Humans Are Coming 69
CHAPTER 4: The Lost Einsteins 91

PART II: WHAT'S CHANGING
CHAPTER 5: Jobs Are Tasks, Not Titles 115
CHAPTER 6: Careers Are Climbing Walls,
   Not Ladders 131
CHAPTER 7: Companies Are Work Charts,
   Not Org Charts 155
CHAPTER 8: Economies Need Innovation,
   from All, for All 181

PART III: THE PATH FORWARD

CHAPTER 9: Nobody Beats You at Being You   205
CHAPTER 10: Open to Work   223

Acknowledgments   249
Notes   251
About the Authors   279

Foreword

It's clear that artificial intelligence is rewriting how we work, learn, and create. From automating the familiar to opening doors to new possibilities, the future is unfolding fast. It's no time to stand still. As the saying goes, 'The secret to getting ahead is getting started.'

This book's title says it all. *Open to Work* is about figuring out *How to Get Ahead in the Age of AI*. Some books offer insights on the impact AI will have on the world. Others help us prepare personally for the impact AI will have on us and our families. In my view, Ryan Roslansky and Aneesh Raman have written the first really good book that does both.

Having worked with Ryan for nearly a decade, I'm not surprised. I've seen firsthand how he consistently combines a deep understanding of technology with a view of its impact on people. One moment he'll be diving into a new product feature to help LinkedIn members find their next job, the next moment he'll be analyzing LinkedIn's economic graph and what it says about where the economy is heading.

This approach combines foresight with pragmatism, giving Ryan the ability to see over the horizon while keeping his feet on the ground. It's a combination we'll all need in the coming years.

In ways that are both beneficial and challenging, we live in a century defined by technological change.

During the first quarter of this century, digital technology transformed almost every aspect of our lives. Mobile devices and cloud services have turned high resolution video conversations from science fiction into an everyday reality. Want to interview for a new job? You're likely to meet a recruiter online before shaking hands. Traveling to a new city? Paper maps feel quaint; instead we tap on an app. From online shopping to streaming entertainment, from real-time document collaboration to instant translation, digital technology has turned what was seemingly impossible into conveniences we take for granted.

As much as the world has changed in the first quarter of this century, it's likely the pace of change between now and 2050 will be even greater. This is because AI, like electricity, is a general purpose technology that will impact every aspect of our economy and society.

There are many causes for optimism. Technology has often made its best contributions when it has reduced toil and fostered creativity. When it has helped thinkers and writers advance scientific discovery and human knowledge. When it has enabled people to connect with each other more closely

Foreword

and come to common understandings. AI can help people do all these things.

But the history of technology shows that the future is also fraught with peril. Almost fifteen decades after Thomas Edison lit his first lightbulb, around seven hundred million people, including close to 50 percent of people in sub-Saharan Africa, still lack access to electricity.[1] This divide, perhaps as much as anything, has contributed to the enormous economic disparity between industrialized countries and the Global South. And the past fifteen years demonstrate how quickly something like social media can evolve from a tool to connect friends into a weapon used by hostile adversaries, including nation-states.

The second half of this decade will pose important questions about where AI is going. For example, are we trying to build machines that are smarter than people, or machines that will help people become smarter? Are we trying to build machines that will outperform people in their jobs, or are we trying to build machines that will help people do more in their jobs? These will be among the most critical questions of our time.

Issues of this magnitude understandably spark both hope and anxiety. AI offers hope for breakthroughs that will cure diseases, personalized learning for students and workers, and relief from the burden of routine and repetitive tasks. But for many, change produces more anxiety than excitement. The questions are reasonable. How will technology impact my job? If AI can do my work better than I can, how will I earn a living? What new skills do I need to develop? Will I be able to learn something so new?

We'll all need a guide to help us answer these questions. This book provides a great start.

One of my favorite chapters describes the technological and societal changes that are reshaping job markets around the world. Employers' traditional focus on credentials has shifted to needing a combination of credentials and capabilities. In other words, knowledge and skills. Pioneered by schools and key universities alike, this has led to changes in both foundational learning and lifelong learning. All this is based on a new synergy between public leadership and private partnerships. These are all trends that we see firsthand across Microsoft and LinkedIn every day.

Success in the age of AI will require the ability for countries, communities, and individuals to navigate these changes. Perhaps most importantly, *Open to Work* provides the types of actionable insights that can equip each of us personally to think keenly and practically about the changes that lie ahead for ourselves, our jobs, our careers, and the places where we'll work.

Like Ryan and Aneesh, I'm optimistic about the new opportunities technology will create. But the age of AI, like prior eras shaped by major technological shifts, will also be disruptive and even unpredictable. In the long run, things have a way of working out. But the path from here to there can be bumpy. We need to ensure that AI advances in ways that put people first, which requires us to be not only well informed but clear-eyed about AI's likely benefits and potential challenges.

Foreword

We will be more successful if we can see a bit farther over the horizon. And then we can better take life one step at a time and keep our feet on the ground.

Brad Smith
Vice Chair and President, Microsoft Corporation

Preface

The world of work is changing faster than any of us could have imagined. Every day, LinkedIn members log in to connect, learn, and build their futures. They come from every corner of the globe. Every industry. Every background. Their stories, your stories, are the pulse of the global economy. Right now, that pulse is quickening.

This book was born from a simple but urgent question: How do we help every member of the LinkedIn community not just survive but succeed in the age of AI? The answer, we believe, is not to predict the future, but to shape it together.

We wrote this book on behalf of all of us at LinkedIn and Microsoft for all of you navigating this moment of historic change. For the nurse in Cleveland using AI to spend more time with patients. For the software engineer in Bangalore learning new skills to stay ahead. For the entrepreneur in Nairobi building a business that did not exist a few years ago. For the college graduate in London asking if the degree she worked so hard to get will open the doors it once did. It's for every person who has ever wondered what comes next for their job, their career, their company, or their community.

The future of work is not a distant horizon. It is being built right now, by people willing to experiment, adapt, and lead. At LinkedIn, we see these changes in real time: new skills emerging, new roles being created, new opportunities opening up for those who are ready to seize them. We also see the anxiety, the uncertainty, and the very real challenges that come with such rapid transformation.

That is why this book is both a road map and a rallying cry. It is a call to action for every member of our community to engage with change, build new capabilities, and help shape a future of work that is more inclusive, innovative, and human.

Aneesh and I could not have written this book alone. Along the way, we have been fortunate to work with people who challenged us to see the world as it is and as it could be. We want to specifically thank three.

First, Jeff Weiner. The CEO of LinkedIn before me, Jeff led this company during a period of profound growth. In the midst of that growth, Jeff kept us tethered to the great opportunity and great responsibility that defines LinkedIn at its core, which is to create economic opportunity for every member of the global workforce. Our growth means nothing if it does not serve the people who depend on us. Jeff's influence can be felt across this book.

Second, Aneesh and I want to thank Steven Stegman. Steven has been at LinkedIn for two decades as a builder and innovator. At a critical moment in the writing of this book, he

Preface

provided guidance that helped us focus on the essential truths of this moment. Steven has a rare gift: He can see the promise of new technology without losing sight of the realities people face every day. His counsel helped us balance optimism with honesty, ambition with humility, and vision with reality. For that, we are deeply grateful.

Lastly, thanks to my daughter, Avery, for showing up with exactly the purpose we needed at exactly the right moment.

The pages that follow are not just about AI, or technology, or even work itself. They are about people, about you, and about the choices we all face in this moment of profound change. Our hope is that this book will help you find your footing, discover your edge, and write your own story into the future of work.

Ryan Roslansky
CEO of LinkedIn and Executive Vice President of Microsoft Office and Copilot

INTRODUCTION

Failure Is Not an Option

Jim Lovell was supposed to walk on the moon.[1] At forty-two, after three missions and after having spent more time in space than any other human alive, this was his moment. His crowning achievement. The story his grandchildren would tell their grandchildren.

Instead, he was two hundred thousand miles above Earth staring at warning lights blazing across a control panel while oxygen hemorrhaged into space.[2]

Beside Lovell was Fred Haise, who had also spent years preparing to leave his footprints in lunar dust, and Jack Swigert, the newcomer. Swigert was still getting his bearings, having stepped in as a last-minute replacement just days before launch.[3]

Fifty-six hours earlier,[4] the voyage to the moon had been unfolding unremarkably. From Mission Control, NASA's nerve center in Houston, the dozens of engineers who monitored every rocket system watched the spacecraft launch on April 11, 1970, at 13:13 military time. Superstitious types noted the timing.

Still, for two days, everything went to plan. Then Mission Control asked for a routine procedure: stir the oxygen tanks to prevent stratification. Jack Swigert flipped the switch.

The bang that followed shook the entire spacecraft. Warning lights erupted across the control panel. Lovell took the mic. 'Houston, we've had a problem.'

Back in Houston, Lovell's voice cut through the static with a chilling detail. 'We are venting something out into space.' That something was oxygen, their lifeline, which was now blowing into the void.[5]

The Mission Control room grew tense. Uncertainty and anxiety filled the air. Everyone was struggling to understand how so many things were going wrong at once. Then flight director Gene Kranz stood up.

'Let's everybody keep cool. Let's solve the problem, but let's not make it any worse by guessing,' he said.[6]

At thirty-six, Kranz was already a legend. The guy with the flattop haircut who wore a different vest made for each mission, he'd guided spacecraft through problems before. While nothing had prepared him for this, he knew that the best thing to do was to break down the process of saving the astronauts, which seemed impossible in the moment, into smaller, more immediate next steps.

How much power remained? What systems could they shut down? Could the lunar module, a spacecraft built for two men for two days, keep three alive for four?

That attitude, which was later captured by Kranz in the title of his autobiography, would define everything about that moment: 'Failure is not an option.'

Failure Is Not an Option

What followed was ninety hours of human innovation. With the guidance of Mission Control, the astronauts turned the lunar module into a lifeboat.[7] Because the square filters from the command module didn't fit the round openings in the lunar module, they built CO_2 scrubbers from duct tape, cardboard, and plastic bags.[8] They oriented themselves by Earth's terminator line, the line that literally separates day and night, because their computer couldn't navigate properly after the explosion.[9] Each solution created new problems. Each problem demanded urgent innovation.

The U.S. president at the time, Richard Nixon, canceled appointments to stay close to updates from NASA. The Soviet Union, a rival in the Space Race, offered assistance.[10] Humanity held its breath together. When the crew splashed down safely in the Pacific Ocean on April 17, the world exhaled.

Why start a book about the future of work with a story from space? Because the triumph of Apollo 13 wasn't just the act of bringing the astronauts home. It proved that in moments of existential crisis, the choice isn't between success and failure; it's between action and paralysis. It's between solving the problem or staring at it. The triumph of Apollo 13 showed, unmistakably, that in moments of crisis, humans can do incredible, even impossible things.

OPEN TO WORK

The Explosion at Work

Today, the changes hitting work can feel like our own Apollo 13 moment.

The explosion was felt all over the world. AI's arrival was both sudden and irreversible. After its release in November 2022, ChatGPT hit one hundred million users in a matter of months, the fastest adoption of any technology in history.[11] Suddenly, technology seemed ready to write, create, and even solve problems in ways previously thought to be uniquely human.

That's when the warning lights started flashing. Software engineers saw AI write code faster, better. Financial analysts saw AI handle complex modeling faster, better. Designers saw AI generate more concepts faster, better.

Experts have spent the past few years trying to predict what's coming for us humans at work, often running across extremes. AI will destroy all jobs! No, it will create new ones! Stop AI! Embrace AI! Retrain everyone! But for what?!

When you hear that, it can all feel decided. Inevitable. As if everything is already figured out and we're just along for the ride. That's especially true when AI is presented as the ultimate efficiency machine, getting faster and better at the very tasks many of us have been training ourselves to master, from the technical to the analytical.

We all have questions right now. Lots of them. Will overall employment go up or down? Which jobs will disappear? Which will endure? Which sectors and societies will surge ahead? Which will struggle? What does this all mean for my job and my career and my way of earning a living? What does this all mean for my students or kids or family or friends?

The truth is, we won't get a lot of those answers for some time, in some cases decades. We don't need those answers, however, to know what to do right now. The most important part of all of this is that those answers are not predetermined. Nothing about this moment is. Where we go next comes down to one thing and one thing only: the choices we make right now as individuals, organizations, economies, and societies.

LinkedIn is the largest professional network the world has ever assembled. We have more than a billion members across more than two hundred countries and territories, spanning tens of millions of companies and schools. Amid all the noise about AI and the future of work, we can see the signals that matter most: skills emerging and evolving, people pivoting and adapting, companies hiring and restructuring, entire industries transforming.

AI isn't the first explosive shift we've seen play out on our platform. Just a few years ago, in June 2020, we launched LinkedIn's Open to Work feature during another such moment. If you're not familiar with it, Open to Work is the little green ring that you can add to your profile picture on LinkedIn to signal that you're open to new job opportunities.

At the time we built it, the world of work was going through the COVID-19 pandemic. Layoffs and job insecurity were rippling across industries of all shapes and sizes. Corporate offices were sending employees home. Main street shops and restaurants were closing their doors, uncertain if and when they'd open again.

The idea behind the feature was simple. There's power in leaning on your community and asking for help when you need it. There's power in having a trusted network to go to during moments of big change. In the last three years, Open to Work has been used by nearly three hundred million members, either publicly on their profiles or privately to notify recruiters.

Today, we find ourselves in another moment of big change, one that will require all of us to be open to new ways of work. Open to building new skills. Open to experimenting with new tools. Open to embarking on new chapters in our careers.

Our colleague Kevin Scott, Microsoft's chief technology officer, made a really important point a few years ago. 'A.I. is one of the most powerful things humans have ever invented for improving the quality of life of everyone. But it will take time. It *should* take time. We've always tackled super-challenging problems through technology. And so we can either tell ourselves a good story about the future or a bad story about the future – and, whichever one we choose, that's probably the one that'll come true.'[12]

On LinkedIn, we see people choosing that good story and inspiring others to join in, not just in believing it but in taking the necessary actions to make it true.

It's clear that we have our work cut out for us. In many ways humanity is running from behind. Across the world, we have to bring greater urgency to helping workers manage what will be, for many, a very difficult moment as their jobs and livelihoods get upended. At the same time, we have to be much more intentional about building a future of work that creates more opportunity for people, not less. That requires all of us, and especially the leaders who will shape the way the systems respond, to engage in more thoughtful debates and discussions.

Impossible, right? Well, that's where Gene Kranz comes in. It's time to focus on the immediate, not the impossible.

This book will show you that the best way to do that is to engage with the change rather than ignore it or wait for it to happen to you. This means trying out AI tools to understand for yourself how they are going to change your work and career, becoming more aware of which skills and jobs are evolving fastest and why, and, ultimately, starting to adapt now before it becomes a necessity rather than a choice.

As for what comes next for work, we should say here that we are pro-human. Our focus at LinkedIn is to create economic opportunity for every member of the global workforce. For every human in the global workforce. So we always start with the goal of helping to unlock the potential that exists in everyone.

That's why, for the past few years, as much of the world has been focused almost entirely on artificial intelligence, we took a different approach and focused with equal curiosity on human intelligence.

Here's what we discovered.

Any focus on artificial intelligence comes with lots of unpredictability. What it can do keeps changing, which jobs it will affect keeps shifting, how quickly it will advance remains unknown. Focusing on human intelligence offers something different. The same brain that has driven every major breakthrough in human history is basically the same brain we have right now. In other words, the foundation for human intelligence hasn't changed for millennia. What has changed, we discovered, is our view of it.

The Real Mission

Across the industrial age, new forms of energy emerged, from steam to electricity. Those new forms of energy supported new forms of technology, from the assembly line to the internet. And with those new forms of technology, economic growth all over the world has increasingly come from one thing above all else: the ability to produce more goods and services, faster and cheaper.

No surprise, then, that the systems of work for us humans became about speed and scale. More, better, faster. More, better, faster. More, better, faster.

As a result, our economies started prizing skills that would support efficiency at scale the most, especially analytical and technical skills. As humans at work, our value was measured by how effectively we could support technology executing more, better, faster. A few of us did work that involved innovating and being entrepreneurial, but for the most part even that work was about creating new goods and services that helped consumers and businesses do more, better, faster.

Failure Is Not an Option

Today we're all mostly manning assembly lines, operating registers, driving tractors, building spreadsheets, writing code, managing meetings, and responding to emails. So. Many. Emails. In every case, across so many of our jobs, our value has been tied to our ability to help organizations achieve that same goal: more output, better quality, faster delivery.

Then came AI.

Suddenly, so much of what we've trained ourselves to do, so much of what our economy has valued most, AI started to do. And it started to do it more efficiently than we ever could, becoming better by the day at precisely the kind of technical and analytical capabilities our economies currently prize above all else. Of course we're worried.

But that fear misses something crucial: Our competitive edge as a species was never our capacity for processing and producing more, better, faster in the first place.

Think about Apollo 13. The astronauts didn't make it home thanks to computational power. They made it home thanks to human innovation. The same is true at work. Efficiency isn't our edge. Innovation is.

As AI starts to handle the 'more, better, faster' work that has consumed so much of our time and energy, we will finally have the opportunity to reclaim the work that only we can do. Work that is based on what makes us uniquely human.

We are the species that tamed fire and built civilization. We took off from Earth and walked on the moon. We decoded DNA and transformed medicine. We've always been able to see what doesn't yet exist and figure out how to make it real. It's just that, for the past few centuries, most of us haven't had the time or training to develop and exercise the skills behind human innovation because we've been too busy doing more, better, faster around what already exists.

What exactly do we mean by human innovation? Think of it as our ability to come up with new ideas and new solutions, even with limited resources. Human innovation is not simply about the major inventions that change the world; it's also about the everyday entrepreneurialism that leads you to look at problems in new ways and make things better than they were before.

With that in mind, we set out to discover which human capabilities allow us to innovate as only we can, and which will be most valuable as AI advances. We spoke to experts on human capability, from neuroscientists to organizational psychologists to talent leaders. Those conversations helped us identify five areas that, when working together, best capture our unique human edge at work: curiosity, courage, creativity, compassion, and communication. We call them the 5Cs.

For decades, the 5Cs have been dismissed as soft skills: nice-to-haves that took a back seat to the hard skills our economy valued most. In the coming years, it will become clear that soft skills are anything but 'soft.' They are the key to our survival. The way work is set up now, however, means we rarely get to draw on them.

How much time do you actually spend bringing those 5Cs into your work? How much time do you actually spend coming up with new solutions to problems? How often do you get to think creatively or try approaches that haven't been done before? Whether you're grading papers, fixing engines, or building spreadsheets, does it ever feel as if you're on an assembly line, rushing to keep up? Does it *always* feel as if you're on an assembly line, rushing to keep up?

As AI takes over efficiency work, we could finally get the time back to do what we do best as humans: being entrepreneurial, on our own and with others.

The possibilities with AI don't stop there, though. AI is not just a force for change; it is also a tool unlike any we've seen before. It can democratize and personalize access to knowledge and expertise for anyone who uses it. It can help turn fragile ideas into working models faster than ever before, helping us all build not just new products and businesses all over the world but entirely new ways of working that value human entrepreneurialism as much as technological efficiency.

AI could be how we flip the script on the last few hundred years and have technology serving us rather than us serving technology. The surest way to deliver on that promise is by distinguishing ourselves from the machine rather than trying to mimic it. Instead of replacing humans at work, we have to believe AI can help us become more human at work.

In that sense, it's not human versus AI; it's human with AI.

Ultimately, we humans get to decide what comes next. The steam engine, electricity, and the internet didn't arrive with set manuals. In each case, the choices humans made about how to deploy them, regulate them, and integrate them into society determined their impact. AI is no different. We're not passive observers waiting to see what happens. We're active participants writing the next chapter for work. And if we choose to use AI to amplify what makes us human rather than replace it, that's the future we'll build.

Making that choice requires action, not just intention. That's why this book offers a framework for navigating the uncertainty, developing AI literacy, fostering adaptability, and deepening the distinctly human capabilities that will matter most.

On LinkedIn, we see people taking these steps all the time, so we're going to tell you some of those stories too. The stories of ordinary people using AI to do new, even extraordinary things at work. They are using AI to do their current job better, to find new jobs more easily, to build new businesses, and, ultimately, to be more human at work. We hope you will be as moved and motivated by them as we are.

Your Mission Control Manual

We've broken down the massive changes ahead into manageable pieces you can tackle one at a time: the Gene Kranz method of taking a seemingly impossible long-term goal and turning it into immediate, actionable steps. With that in mind, the book builds across three sections.

Part I: The Wake-Up Call confronts our very human fear of change and shows how, for centuries, work has been anchored around efficiency and therefore limited our ability to bring our full human potential to bear. This section reveals how one of our key competitive advantages as a species has always been the ability to innovate, and introduces the 5Cs as the distinctly human capabilities that AI cannot replicate. Finally, it explains how millions of us, the 'Lost Einsteins,' have been excluded from the arena of innovation, and why the AI era offers an unprecedented opportunity to unlock entrepreneurialism and innovation at scale.

Part II: What's Changing gives you a way to apply the big changes we describe in the first section to your everyday work life. Your job isn't a title anymore; it's a portfolio of tasks that will shift constantly. Your career is no longer a ladder; it's a climbing wall you can scale in any direction. Your company can't stay a rigid hierarchy organized around predictability and efficiency; it needs to organize around adaptability and innovation. The economy can't chase efficiency alone; it will also need to support entrepreneurialism coming from all people and places.

Part III: The Path Forward moves from understanding to action. We show how embracing your individuality will become a further edge when AI handles everything generic. Finally, we provide you with a tactical tool kit, a 30-60-90-day plan, to turn any lingering anxiety into agency and, over time, perhaps even aspiration about the opportunities that lie ahead for you.

The Choice

'Failure is not an option' wasn't just a catchphrase or the title of Gene Kranz's book. It was a very intentional choice. A decision to believe that solutions existed even if they weren't yet apparent. A commitment to keep working until human ingenuity found them.

You face the same choice now. The explosion has happened. The oxygen of old work is venting into space. The fear is real. But failure isn't inevitable.

As Gene Kranz understood that night in Mission Control, you don't need perfect solutions. You just need to start solving. You don't need to see the whole path. You just need to take the first step. Then the next step. You don't need to beat fear. You just need to act despite it.

The Apollo 13 crew made it home because hundreds of people worked to solve the problem instead of agonizing over it. As we were writing this book, Jim Lovell passed away at ninety-seven years old. His obituary in *The New York Times* ended with this quotation from an interview he had given decades earlier: 'I realized that although I didn't land on the moon and was disappointed, it was a triumph in a different direction, meaning getting people back from a certain catastrophe.'[13]

Now it's our turn, not to save a mission but to save something just as vital: the idea that there will always be a place for humans at work because our capabilities are unique and our ingenuity irreplaceable. If we do that, the work ahead will be far better than the work we leave behind.

PART I

THE WAKE-UP CALL

CHAPTER 1

Buckle Up

Here's the deal. AI won't replace you at work, but someone using AI likely will. Maybe not today or tomorrow. Maybe not this year or even next. But eventually. And if you wait for eventually, it will be too late.

For some, that shift is already happening. A recent 'Work Change Report' from LinkedIn found that nearly 90 percent of C-suite leaders say accelerating AI adoption is critical.[1] Not just someday. Now. Together with Microsoft, we also found that a new hiring calculus is locking in, with two-thirds of corporate leaders saying they won't even consider candidates without AI skills.[2]

This is just the beginning. Ask leaders who truly understand AI about the years ahead, and they don't talk about tweaks or upgrades. They talk about reimagining work entirely.

This thinking isn't just true in tech circles. As early as 2023, one-third of content writers on LinkedIn had added AI literacy skills to their profiles, significantly outpacing software engineers at 19 percent. Graphic designers (27 percent) and marketing managers (24 percent) showed similar enthusiasm for building AI literacy.[3] By early 2025 AI literacy had become one of the skills LinkedIn members from all over the world added most to their profiles.[4]

Out there right now, a real estate agent is using AI to help write property descriptions and manage scheduling, freeing up more time to walk potential buyers through homes and help them envision raising a family there. A retail manager is using AI to help decode buying patterns and predict seasonal shifts, creating space to build deeper relationships with suppliers and customers. A small business owner is using AI to help handle bookkeeping and social media, giving them time to develop new products and personally serve their most important customers.

Workers in every field are using AI right now. As they're doing that, they're learning which parts of their jobs AI can do and what that means for their future. The data is striking: Researchers at LinkedIn found that 24 percent of skills for the average job changed globally from 2015 to 2022.[5] As we look ahead to 2030 and consider the impact of AI, we estimate that this proportion will jump to as high as 70 percent.

What does all this mean for you? It means your job is changing on you even if you aren't changing jobs. And right this moment, while you're reading these words, people who do jobs just like yours are out there trying things out with AI. They're not waiting for permission. They're not waiting for someone else to go first. They're open to solving the problem as it's changing. Open to learning, testing, building, and getting better. Every day.

They understand perhaps the most important things about this moment. First, change at work will never be as slow as it is now. Second, AI as a tool will never be as basic as it is now. Third, every day you wait, the gap between those experimenting with AI and those hesitating widens.

The reason that gap is growing is because of something unique about AI: The technology gets better at understanding you while you get better at understanding it. Every interaction is a two-way upgrade. It's like riding a bicycle that understands you better the more you ride. The pedals start to match your rhythm. The seat adjusts to support you better. The handlebars find the perfect position for your reach. Each improvement removes resistance and difficulty. Every mile makes the next mile easier, until you're gliding along on a bike that can kind of feel like an extension of yourself.

That's the individual experience. Zoom out, and you'll see something bigger happening.

Understanding the S-Curve of Change

There's a pattern to big, technological change like this.[6] It's called an S-curve.

Picture it like this: New technologies start slowly, almost invisibly. For years, they seem like toys or niche tools that only enthusiasts care about. That's the bottom of the S-curve, where progress crawls. During that time, most people feel comfortable ignoring it. The internet in 1993. Social media in 2004. AI in 2020.

Then something shifts. The technology hits a tipping point and suddenly shoots upward. That's the steep middle of the S-curve where everything starts happening fast. Adoption explodes. Industries transform. The people who dismissed it as hype now race to catch up. Finally, eventually, growth plateaus at the top of the S-curve as the technology becomes common infrastructure. It becomes as essential and unremarkable as electricity or running water.

AI isn't at the bottom of the S-curve anymore. The hundred-million-user mark for ChatGPT was the S-curve starting to bend upward. Which means we're entering the steep part where adoption stops being optional.

In the past, one of the understandable concerns that held people back from experimenting with a new technology was that using it initially felt like cheating. Scribes believed the printing press would bring an end to learning.[7] Calculators were a threat to understanding basic math. Spellcheck was suspect. Googling things was lazy. Each time, the accusation was the same: Using this tool means you're not really doing the work.

For decades now, the time it has taken us to get through the steep part of an S-Curve has been decreasing, which means that each generation of technology has given us less time to adapt than the last. Humans had decades to process the arrival of electricity and television, years to adjust to the internet and smartphones. Now, with AI, we have months, sometimes weeks, before the next breakthrough feels like it is advancing everything again.

The change is happening faster than our brains can truly process. Humans think linearly. We expect tomorrow to resemble yesterday, maybe with a few tweaks. It's how we survived for millennia, recognizing patterns, building on experience, making incremental improvements. Like following a trail through the forest, each step builds on the last, and we assume the path ahead will generally look like the path behind.

That isn't how technology builds or spreads.

Consider photography. For a hundred years, taking more photos meant buying more film. Linear growth. Then digital cameras arrived. Suddenly taking a thousand photos cost the same as taking one. By 2000, humanity took eighty billion photos per year.[8] By 2024? Worldwide, we take that many every few weeks. Billions of photos every day. And we crop, edit, copy, and share them at will. That's exponential change. It's not just more, but fundamentally different.

This mismatch between how we expect the world to look and how technology develops creates a dangerous gap. Our brains evolved to witness change unfold over decades, even centuries. Now massive change happens in years, sometimes months. And here's why that's so hard for us to manage: Fear of change is a real thing for humans, and it isn't a weakness. It's biology.

When you feel that knot in your stomach thinking about AI, when your chest tightens reading about jobs getting disrupted, when you want to dismiss this all as hype, that's not you being difficult. That's millions of years of evolution trying to keep you safe.

At work, our amygdala, which is the brain's alarm system that kept our ancestors from becoming prey, can't tell the difference between a rapidly charging lion and a rapidly changing technology. Both trigger the same response: freeze, fight, or flee. When faced with AI, many workers are doing exactly what their biology demands: freezing in place, fighting the technology, or fleeing to familiar ground.

So, if you haven't started experimenting with AI yet, you're not flawed. You're experiencing the very human fear of the unknown. Not just professionally, but existentially. What if your skills don't matter anymore? What if who you are doesn't matter? That's the fear beneath the fear: not just the loss of a job, but the loss of a livelihood and an identity.

Understanding this helps. You're not broken if you feel overwhelmed. You're human. But being human at work right now means overriding instincts that no longer serve you. And fast.

The Red Queen's Warning

In Lewis Carroll's *Through the Looking-Glass, and What Alice Found There*, the Red Queen tells Alice: 'Now, *here*, you see, it takes all the running *you* can do, to keep in the same place. If you want to get somewhere else, you must run at least twice as fast as that!'[9]

That line from a children's book works as a principle for survival in rapidly changing environments. And it highlights another challenge of managing big change, which is that even after we've felt the ground shifting beneath our feet, our instinct is often to hunker down. But when everything around you is evolving, standing still means falling behind.

Think about competitive environments where both sides constantly adapt. In baseball, today's hitters use video analysis and launch-angle training to perfect their swings. But they're not dominating the game. Pitchers can now throw faster than ever, armed with detailed data on every batter's weakness. Neither side can rest. The moment one stops innovating, the other pulls ahead.

The same scenario unfolds everywhere competition exists. Cybersecurity experts develop new protections just as hackers find new vulnerabilities. Investors spot undervalued opportunities but as soon as they act, the market adjusts and prices in that information. Every move triggers a countermove.

You're probably experiencing this same pressure without realizing it. At work, falling behind rarely feels swift or dramatic. It can feel more casual, more incremental, even easy to miss.

Maybe a colleague is suddenly talking about tools you haven't heard about. Or job postings for a role similar to yours start listing requirements that didn't exist a few years ago. Or there's a meeting where you realize everyone else seems to be speaking a slightly different language, talking about new approaches that feel foreign.

Importantly, the dynamic that's playing out isn't one that pits you against other workers. You're racing against the drastic transformation of work itself. While you may be holding on to familiar skills and proven methods, work is changing at a fundamental level, which is why, since 2022, the rate at which LinkedIn members have been adding new skills to their profiles has increased by 140 percent.[10] Many of us are constantly upskilling, or reconsidering which of our skills matter in the changing world of work.

So how, precisely, do you move forward? It's not just about experimenting with AI. It's about using AI to amplify what makes you unique.

What You Bring to the Table

Ume Habiba is a friendly, outgoing twenty-something who is a software engineer at Microsoft. She also happens to have more than eighty-five thousand followers on Instagram, where she posts videos about how to code. Ume has a lifelong passion for fashion and often draws on clothing items as props and metaphors to explain complex coding problems.[11]

Ume first heard about AI when she was in the fall semester of her junior year at the University of Maryland. As an information sciences major, she was constantly encouraged by classmates to experiment with AI. But she wasn't all that interested. 'How groundbreaking can this really be?' she thought at the time.

Then, the following semester, she started playing around a little to see if it could help her with her homework. She soon discovered that so much of what she had spent years learning in class could be done by AI. The coursework she had worked hard to master was, to use her word, 'busywork.'

'It's really just work that you can plug into ChatGPT or Claude or Copilot and ask it to do. And there's your discus-

Buckle Up

sion post,' Ume says. 'After I graduated, I reflected on my four and a half years at Maryland, and I thought, "Hey, my last two years, they easily could have just been plugged into ChatGPT. And I could have just graduated."'

Most people would have a crisis at this point. Not Ume.

Ume immigrated to America with her family as a young child. She grew up in a low-income household in Dundalk, Maryland. The friendly, outgoing Ume of today, the girl with more than eighty-five thousand followers, says that she was 'the shyest girl in the room' at her elementary school. Then she had a chance to go to a magnet middle school outside her district.

'No one from my elementary school went to that middle school. I was put into a position where I couldn't be shy anymore. I had to put myself out there,' Ume says.

The exposure to so many kids from other backgrounds made Ume realize that 'there was so much to the world that was out there, that I wanted to discover and I wanted to learn more about. And I would only be able to do that if I took risks and said yes to things that made me scared, said yes to things that seemed way out of my potential or bracket, and just learned how to fail. And that was something that I was always very scared of. I was always scared of failing because I didn't want to disappoint my immigrant parents.'

By putting herself out there, taking risks and failing, Ume realized that she actually wasn't shy. She was a people person.

And so, by the time she realized that AI could do much of what she'd been asked to do in her classes, she wasn't frightened because, as she says, 'I just knew that what was going to take me far wasn't being the smartest person in the room, wasn't that I knew the most insane algorithms and I could code anything you told me to. What was going to set me apart was the fact that, one, I was willing to learn and, two, I was willing to converse and be a people person.

'I always say AI is not going to take over my job, because I know what I bring to the table that AI cannot,' Ume says. 'Soft skills are so much more than "I can talk to a person." It's being kind to people. It's showing compassion and being able to offer those human aspects that AI just can't. And you have to be able to use AI and bridge those soft skills that you bring and then bridge AI in order to produce something that no one else is bringing to the table.'

For Ume, AI is a valuable partner on the content she produces, but she remains the executive. What AI saves her is *time*, taking over some of the technical work of making content so that she can be more creative and more genuine and ultimately reach more people.

'First, I think one of the most important things is knowing how to prompt AI,' Ume says. 'It's important to provide context, and so I provide context on who I am, what kind of content I create, what I'm focused on, and what I want AI to do, and then I tell it to internalize this information, and then I'll tell it what to do next.'

After this step, Ume tells her AI tool what kind of content she wants to create for a particular video. Then she plugs in her personal breakdowns of coding problems, basically solutions she's come to on her own without the help of AI, so that AI can see how her brain works.

Buckle Up

At that point, she tells the tool, 'Now, can you put this into an analogy that is relatable to young girls, that is easy to understand, but also uses a step-by-step breakdown that I just mentioned, making sure that you use all of that context that I provided, all of those products that I already own?'

The result is remarkably and consistently good. Ume says that 90 percent of the time AI produces an analogy that is almost perfect. If not, she asks it to do it again. If not, a third time. By the third time, it's ideal. That's time saved that Ume can spend crafting more creative ways to reach her audience or thinking about how to more deeply connect with her followers.

She also always takes the time, she says, to revise what AI generates to 'make it into my words or my style. Because AI is still very monotone, and so I like to make it a little bit more energetic.'

AI helps Ume craft her analogies and further her mission of getting girls interested in computer science. It does not replace her. It does the work alongside her, for her. It allows her to create more videos and reach more people. And it frees her to do the things that matter most, allowing her to spend her time thinking creatively rather than doing routine work.

Ultimately, Ume says, it's her authentic self that people are coming to the videos for. Not just the information. 'They're getting Ume; they're getting Ume speaking to the screen because that's what catches my community's attention.'

OPEN TO WORK

Don't Fight the Future

In 1811, bands of skilled weavers across England began destroying the mechanical looms that threatened their livelihoods.[12] When questioned, the weavers blamed the damage on a mysterious man called Ned Ludd. Ned Ludd was a Robin Hood figure, a fictional leader for a real rebellion, a name to hide behind while they fought the future.

The Luddites, as they came to be known, weren't skeptical of technology. They believed in it. And that's why they were desperate. They were master craftsmen who understood exactly what the new machines meant: the end of their ability to earn a living. They could see the future clearly. They just thought they could stop it.

Ultimately, this is the hard truth of technological resistance. Those who fight hardest against change often understand its immediate consequences best. They see clearly what will be lost. When it comes to work, they aren't focused on what might be gained.

MIT studied this pattern and found that 60 percent of the jobs we were doing in 2018 did not exist in 1940.[13] More recently, LinkedIn found that nearly 70 percent of the jobs on the United States 2024 Jobs on the Rise List didn't exist twenty years ago. The lesson? Technology doesn't just replace work; it transforms what work can be, creating new jobs and new job categories in the process.

While the Luddites grasped what they stood to lose, they couldn't see the new jobs to come, like mechanic, engineer, and designer.

Buckle Up

The scribes who opposed Gutenberg's printing press in 1450? Within fifty years, Europe had nine million books[14] in circulation, more than had been produced in the previous thousand years combined. All those books created all kinds of new jobs like typesetter, printer, and bookbinder.

The telephone operators who resisted automated switching? By 1950, there were more people working in telecommunications than ever before. They just did different jobs.

It's important here for us to be clear about something: Recognizing historical patterns doesn't diminish the very real pain of disruption. The Luddites weren't wrong to be worried about their own particular jobs and livelihoods. Nor were the scribes or operators. They all had families to feed, skills that took decades to master, communities built around their craft, identities based on their workmanship.

When technology comes for your ability to make money, telling you about potential future jobs offers little comfort. The Luddites whose jobs vanished lost their livelihoods, and they personally did not benefit from the textile industry that replaced them. Yes, new jobs were created, but the workers themselves had little control over their fate. No advance warning. No tools to help them adapt. This is a truth across history, but it doesn't need to repeat itself.

This time, the knowledge of what's changing is available to everyone, and the ability to manage the change is available to everyone who has access to AI tools. And, critically, we still have time to adapt before AI fully transforms our jobs and industries.

OPEN TO WORK

You Can Learn New Tricks

'I'm the old dog that learned the new trick,' says Jonetta Gresham,[15] a fifty-something nurse turned project manager. 'And AI is the new trick.'

The distance from Luddite to AI advocate might feel like a stretch. Across the globe, though, people like Jonetta are making that leap daily. Not simply because they have to, but because they believe that this new technology could perhaps make them better at what they do.

Jonetta's vision for her career began early. Growing up in a low-income neighborhood in Cincinnati, Jonetta admired her mother's work ethic, but she also wanted to have a different kind of working life from her mother. 'I did not want to work a job. I wanted to have a career ... I felt like my mother was working a job.'

So Jonetta worked as a nurse for many decades. Then one of her children needed her at home, and so she pivoted to various kinds of contract work. By the time she was reentering the workforce and thinking about a move into technology, AI was emerging. Jonetta was more than a little skeptical.

'I was the "hell no to AI" person,' Jonetta says, laughing. She remembers thinking, 'What is that? Why would I be using that?'

'But,' she says with a smile, 'the minute I started using it, I haven't stopped.' She pauses for emphasis, slowly repeating each word, 'I. Have. Not. Stopped.'

Buckle Up

Growing up in the 1970s and 1980s had given Jonetta plenty of reasons to fear machines. 'We had *The Terminator*, and we had *Star Wars*, and we had all of those things that were on the big screen that said hell no to the machine. Plus, I read George Orwell's *1984*.'

Today, Jonetta manages digital health projects, overseeing electronic medical record training for clinicians. Her transformation into an AI advocate began during a course offered by Merit America, a nonprofit that offers pathways for Americans working in low-wage jobs. The assignment was simple: to create a résumé using AI.

'This is *me* on paper,' Jonetta remembers thinking when she saw the result. 'It leveraged my skills.'

That moment changed everything. AI wasn't replacing her thinking. It was showing her new ways to tell her story. Now, she uses it all the time for this purpose.

'When you have to change your résumé to fit a role, you know how much work that is? Just to take the skills you've got and fit them into a format that matches the job you're seeking?'

AI saves her time and helps her better explain what makes her irreplaceable. In fact, AI has changed Jonetta's view of her own mind in a way that she says feels liberating.

Ever since she was young, Jonetta has always had an extraordinary memory. As a child, she would read *TV Guide*. 'What's coming on next?' her family would ask. Jonetta always knew the answer.

But Jonetta didn't want the focus of her work to be memorizing facts. She craved thinking work: making sense of information, solving complex problems, bringing critical thinking to the tasks at hand.

AI has allowed her to spend less time relying on her memory for facts and more time figuring out what those facts really mean.

When studying for an IT certification, Jonetta trained an AI tool on her voice and thought process. She then used AI to explain the material using terms she would use and analogies she could understand. Instead of simply memorizing the information, she found that using AI to personalize the material to her learning style meant that she 'could actually get it.'

She passed the test. More importantly, she'd found an approach to this new tool: AI as an ally, not an adversary.

AI 101

If you're skeptical about AI, we get it. If you're tired of hearing about AI, we get it. If you feel as if you need to nod in agreement when someone talks about AI even though you have no idea what they're talking about, we get that too.

Here's the good news: In order to get ahead in the age of AI, you don't need to build AI. You just need to know how to use it. You've probably done something like this before. At some point you likely learned how to type, send emails, make a PowerPoint deck, and work a smartphone. None of that required that you learn how to build a computer or write code. For the vast majority of us, this is the same process, except this time the way you work with this tool is by talking to it like you would another person.

So what is AI, really? A simple way to think about it is as a technology that can do things we previously thought were not possible for machines: learning from experience, parsing language, generating content. AI learns by processing enormous amounts of data from books, articles, code, conversations, and images. It then identifies the relationships between them. When you use ChatGPT or Copilot, you're interacting with what's called a large language model (LLM): a system that doesn't just memorize facts but understands context well enough to write an email, debug code, or do the first draft of a strategy memo.

And it's getting more capable. These AI systems are evolving into 'agents.' You may have heard that term recently. It just means tools that don't simply respond to requests but can take action, make decisions, and complete multistep tasks with minimal or no human oversight.

The most important thing to remember about AI is that you don't need to understand how it works under the hood. You just need to start using it.

The Only Way Out Is Through

So here we are. You understand the speed of change. You also get that understanding isn't enough. You need a way to manage it.

This book is that way. It's not a rigid playbook, since those don't work when the game keeps changing. Instead, this book will show you how to build what actually matters: the mindset and moves that allow for greater control in the midst of disruption.

If Ume's attitude that AI cannot replace her feels foreign to you, don't worry. Soon it won't. If Jonetta's journey from skeptic to advocate seems impossible to replicate, don't worry. We'll show you how to get there, and how to make the journey your own.

The point is that the workers getting ahead aren't necessarily the most resourced or technical. They're the ones who experiment before they must. Not frantically, but with intention. They practice adapting before they have to. They know that learning *how* to learn matters more than what you currently know. Use Ume's words as a motto. What set her apart? She was 'willing to learn.'

When Ume and Jonetta started experimenting with AI, they discovered something profound: They could use AI to amplify their unique human capabilities. They didn't hold on to careers or frameworks that no longer served them. They chose curiosity over comfort. They prioritized the possibilities of new work over the 'this is how it's always done' mindset.

Which brings us to something crucial: The old ways of work weren't designed to unleash human potential. They were designed for industrial efficiency. For speed. For scale. For predictability. For us humans to do more, better, faster.

That old world is coming apart. And that's actually the opportunity.

For the first time in centuries, we can build work around what makes us most human: our capacity to create, solve novel problems, and connect meaningfully. AI handles the efficiency work. That frees us to do what no algorithm can: create solutions that have never existed before. And yet, so many of us are still holding on to the old rules.

That's where we're going in the next chapter. Because before you can build something better, you need to give yourself permission to let go of what isn't working. Especially if it's all you've ever known.

The Bottom Line

1. **The pace of change is exponential, not linear.** Change will never be this slow again. AI will never be this basic again. The time to experiment is now.

2. **Your resistance is biology, not weakness.** That knot in your stomach when you think about AI? That's millions of years of evolution trying to protect you from rapid change. But the instincts that once kept you safe could now keep you stuck.

3. **Don't fight the future; build it.** Technology doesn't just replace old work; it transforms what work can be. Those who resist change see only what might be lost. Those who adapt are able to see what can be gained.

CHAPTER 2

Let It Go

Before there were alarm clocks, there was Mary Smith and her peashooter.[1] Every morning in early twentieth-century London, she grabbed her tool and walked the streets, shooting dried peas at bedroom windows to wake up workers for their shifts.[2] She was called a knocker-upper and was one of many who served as a human alarm clock before mechanical ones became available.

For decades, this was honest work. Knocker-uppers established territories and refined techniques. Mary perfected her peashooter method. Others used long poles or threw pebbles. They took pride in never missing a wake-up call. In industrial towns across England, entire neighborhoods relied on their morning tap-tap-tap to start the day.

When affordable alarm clocks arrived in the 1920s, the knocker-uppers' days were numbered. One by one, their customers bought clocks instead. Why pay someone weekly when a reliable, cheap alarm clock was available? Within a generation, a profession that had existed for decades was disappearing.

OPEN TO WORK

Mary needed that job. Every penny mattered for keeping food on the table and a roof overhead. But needing the work and questioning the need for that work to be done by human hands and minds aren't mutually exclusive. The missed opportunity wasn't the work itself, but that the world of work funneled all of Mary Smith's potential into a single repetitive task.

Today, to some degree or another, we're all Mary Smith. The financial analyst formatting spreadsheets for hours each week. The mechanic spending more time filling out warranty paperwork than coming up with ways to fix engines. The health care worker typing notes instead of tending to patients. Each doing necessary work but work that isn't us at our most capable.

This didn't happen by accident. It happened by design.

How We Got Here

For thousands of years, work had a certain pace and rhythm to it. Craftsmen made things by hand. Farmers worked with the seasons. Merchants traveled routes that had existed for generations. Work was personal, varied, and deeply human. Skills passed from master to apprentice over decades, and each craftsman brought their own judgment, creativity, and relationships to their trade.

Then came the factories.

Consider a village shoemaker in 1800. He worked in a small shop, perhaps attached to his home. He knew every customer, chose his own hours, took breaks when he needed them, and took real pride in creating boots that would last years, sometimes decades. It took him about a day to make a pair of shoes. Each pair was unique: shaped by his hands, his experience, and his relationship with the person who would wear them.

The village shoemaker's job was closer to a kind of craftsmanship, woven into the fabric of the community. The shoemaker had time to think about individual needs, to experiment with new techniques, and to invent custom solutions for challenging fits. His value came from his ability to solve problems in novel ways and to create something suited to people he knew personally.

By the 1920s, so much of this had changed. The largest shoe factories[3] employed thousands of workers and could produce tens of thousands of pairs daily. Those thousands of workers weren't like the shoemakers of old. They were human components in a mechanical system, each performing one task hundreds of times per day, every day, for years. One person cut leather. Another attached soles. A third applied finishing. No one knew the customers who would wear them.

Why did this happen? The logic was simple. Machines could produce more shoes of more consistent quality faster than any craftsman ever could. More output meant lower costs, cheaper products, and bigger profits. So humans had to work faster, more predictably, and more like the machines they supported. Markets and consumers rewarded efficiency above all else.

There was a real human cost to this transformation and, to be clear, there has always been a human cost to work. Labor, for many humans across history, has been brutal.[4] Hours long, protections absent, agency and economic security scarce.[5] With factories, children were working long hours in dangerous conditions.[6] Workers were losing fingers, hands, even their lives to unguarded machinery.[7] The air was thick with dust or ash, destroying lungs. There were often no sick days and few safety standards; instead, there was a relentless focus on production. It ultimately took generations of strikes, protests, and hard-won legislation to secure new protections.[8]

As the industrial age matured and regulations were put in place, the era eventually produced big innovations, leading to real improvements in the quality of life. In 1820, eight out of ten people lived in what we'd now call extreme poverty.[9] Life expectancy barely reached thirty.[10] Most people couldn't read,[11] and many watched their children die before age five.[12] The industrial age helped us to deliver mass-produced life-saving medicines, distribute food at unprecedented scale, and make education more widely accessible than ever before. Today, extreme poverty affects less than one in ten people globally.[13] Global literacy is close to 90 percent.[14] We live past seventy on average.[15]

Over time, the focus on efficiency became an economic reality. The best worker was the one who made the machines run most efficiently, whether he was operating equipment on the factory floor or managing the workers and optimizing their efficiency. This assumption didn't stay in the factories. As the economy evolved from making goods to processing information, we simply transferred the same thinking to office buildings.

Let It Go

The result was inevitable. We built workplace systems designed to make human behavior as predictable and measurable as the machines we served. These systems perhaps made sense when work was mechanical and stable, but they became so entrenched that we kept them long after work itself started changing.

Take the idea that everyone must be in the same place at the same time from nine to five every weekday. That idea made sense in factories given that assembly lines literally couldn't run unless workers stood at their stations simultaneously, passing parts from one person to the next. The machinery demanded synchronized presence. Workers fought for an eight-hour day throughout the late 1800s; Henry Ford introduced it in the early 1900s.[16] By the post-World War II era, the nine-to-five weekday became the norm.

When work shifted from factories to offices, we carried the old rules with us, still believing that everyone needed to be in the same place at the same time. As projects started to span multiple buildings, cities, and countries, requiring teams to collaborate across time zones and borders, we started to question that belief. Thanks to new tools, people working anywhere at any hour could collaborate on shared documents and communicate online, freeing us up from the requirement of working simultaneously.

In 2020, the pandemic upended work and forced companies to finally take a hard look at some of these rituals. Between April and December 2020, 50 percent of paid work hours in the United States were done via telework, compared with just 5 percent pre-pandemic.[17] Productivity often went up, not down. Meetings that 'couldn't possibly' be emails became emails. The forced experiment revealed that many of our work rituals weren't about work at all. They were about tradition and the comfort of familiarity. How often have you heard someone at work say, 'This is how we've always done it'?

As we emerged from the pandemic, some companies pulled people back to the office; others doubled down on remote work. Others still are attempting hybrid models. Each organization is trying to figure out what drives innovation, collaboration, and culture. The answers vary wildly because humans vary wildly. What works for a startup in Seoul might fail for a bank in London. What energizes a team of accountants might exhaust a team of marketers.

What the pandemic revealed about rituals was only the surface. Beneath them sits something sturdier, a system we rarely question: the collar system. If rituals told us how to work, collars told us what we were worth for doing that work.

The Stacking

In the early 1900s, you could tell where someone worked by looking at their collar. Walk into any city office and you'd see rows of starched white shirts, which signaled work done at a desk with papers and ledgers. Walk into a factory and you'd see blue denim: durable cloth that could withstand the physical demands of production lines and machine shops.

The colors eventually became a sorting system. 'White collar' emerged as a shorthand for office workers, managers, and professionals, basically for people whose labor meant managing information indoors. 'Blue collar' followed for factory workers and tradespeople whose work meant making and building things. By the 1970s, we'd added 'pink collar' for teaching, nursing, and secretarial work, which were roles that required advanced interpersonal and caregiving skills and tended to be done by women.[18]

White-collar work became a cultural aspiration. The closer you were to designing and managing the businesses themselves, the more valuable you were and the better paid you would become. Blue collars applied their physical abilities to produce material goods as efficiently as possible. Pink collars offered their emotional labor to process human needs as efficiently as possible. Meanwhile, white collars channeled their intellect to design, manage, and scale businesses and industries.

White-collar work promised an escape. Get the right education and you get to use your mind. With a white-collar job you could create instead of execute. Innovate instead of repeat. That was the promise. It never really panned out, though. In the end, white-collar work, for most, just brought the factory's focus on efficiency into the office.

Within white-collar work, advanced degrees became the ultimate marker of status. The MBA, created by Harvard in the early 1900s,[19] became a rite of passage for corporate leadership by teaching standardized frameworks and processes designed to maximize organizational efficiency. Students learned to understand financial structures and human resources as well as optimize supply chains, all in service of producing more output, better quality, faster delivery.

OPEN TO WORK

To be sure, this era produced genuine business innovation: new financial instruments, global supply chains, management theories that reorganized work at an unprecedented scale. Visionaries completely reimagined what companies could do and how they could function.

Most MBA graduates, however, weren't trained to be entrepreneurial, nor given the time to be innovative. For every executive reshaping an industry, there were thousands of managers implementing standardized processes, following decision trees, and improving existing systems to squeeze out efficiency gains. The white-collar workforce expanded not because companies needed more imaginative thinkers but because they needed more people to execute increasingly complex administrative tasks, all designed around the same goal of doing more, better, faster.

More recently, computer science degrees and programming jobs have claimed the top spot on the white-collar pyramid, bringing with them the same implicit promise: Master these skills and you'll be the one doing the thinking, the creating.

Again, the tech sector has produced unprecedented innovation, from the internet to smartphones to e-commerce. And the rise of Silicon Valley and the focus on entrepreneurialism it created did dramatically expand the playing field when it came to innovation. Startups were launching out of garages and eventually becoming multinational corporations.

But, for the vast majority of people, the efficiency pattern held. For every visionary who had the wherewithal to successfully launch a startup, for every breakthrough in software or hardware, there were armies of developers building, optimizing, and maintaining the systems. The sector rewarded engineers with the highest salaries precisely because they excelled at logical, systematic thinking, turning creative concepts into executable code as efficiently as possible.

So, ultimately, even at the top of the collar hierarchy, in those computer science jobs, the efficiency focus persisted. The goal was still more, better, faster. More code written. Better algorithms optimized. Faster systems delivered.

Which brings us to AI.

The Reality of White-Collar Work

LinkedIn's research team recently analyzed more than five hundred skills likely to be affected by AI. When we looked specifically at software engineers, our finding was stark: The vast majority of a software engineer's current skills, particularly their proficiency in programming languages, could eventually be replicated by AI.[20]

Think about that. The very skills we've been telling people to master, the ones commanding six-figure starting salaries, are shaping up to be precisely the kind of thing AI does best.

As we wrote this book, a headline in *The New York Times* read, 'Goodbye, $165,000 Tech Jobs. Student Coders Seek Work at Chipotle.'[21] The Federal Reserve Bank of New York found that some of the highest unemployment rates for recent college graduates, people aged twenty-two to twenty-seven, were computer science and computer engineering majors.[22]

OPEN TO WORK

Software engineers won't face this moment of big change alone. To some degree, the shifts they are seeing will be true across white-collar work, especially for roles centered on processing or analyzing information.

Our research finds that 85 percent of LinkedIn members are in jobs that could leverage AI to automate at least a quarter of routine tasks.[23] The jobs most likely to evolve soonest include software engineers but also data analysts, accountants, and web designers.

Underneath those early signs of disruption is the true reality of the white-collar workday. According to research by Asana, 60 percent of a person's time at work is spent on work 'about work,' which they define as tasks like chasing updates, attending unnecessary meetings, and switching between tools. Microsoft data has shown that the average white-collar worker receives more than a hundred emails daily, most of them skimmed in under sixty seconds.[24]

Here's what all this reveals: White-collar work was supposed to be different. It was often presented as an escape from the assembly line, the place where ingenuity would finally matter more than efficiency. Somehow, we ended up building a different kind of assembly line in white-collar work: one where workers process information instead of parts, where thinking got replaced by emails, where innovation became a buzzword while most of the day went to meetings and meetings about meetings.

In the end, the hierarchy of collars was always kind of a myth. White-collar work wasn't more valuable because it unleashed human capability more fully. It was more valuable because it sat closer to the systems that brought efficiency to everything else.

Anne-Marie Slaughter[25] is the CEO and president of New America, a think tank with a mission of 'realizing the promise of America in an era of rapid technological and social change.' A globally recognized scholar and thinker, she puts it this way: 'AI is the first technology that is actually going to take knowledge jobs rather than manual labor.' That isn't because AI is smarter than humans. It's because most of those jobs haven't actually allowed for much real thinking for a long time.

Workers are already recognizing this shift. Young people are starting to choose blue-collar careers, with growing enrollment in vocational programs for welding, construction, and electrical work.[26] Recent graduates are opting for apprenticeships over student debt, skilled trades over spreadsheets.

The reasons are pragmatic. Skilled tradespeople, like plumbers and electricians, can now earn competitive wages, sometimes exceeding those of office workers, while avoiding the burden of student loans that accompany the degrees often needed to get those office jobs. Blue-collar jobs require physical presence and situational problem-solving that technology cannot easily replicate. At least not yet.

And it's not just about what AI can't do. It's also about what humans need. Anne-Marie sees this moment as potentially transformational, especially for traditionally undervalued work like caregiving, teaching, and nursing, all part of what she calls the New Care Economy: 'We have a once-in-a-lifetime, once-in-a-century, once-in-a-millennium opportunity to lift up jobs that depend on human relationships and connection and value them financially and socially.'

The hierarchy we've lived with for generations is getting upended before our eyes. The work that requires human presence, judgment in context, and relationships turns out to be exactly what AI can't replicate, whether that's a plumber diagnosing a mysterious leak, a nurse comforting a frightened patient, or a teacher reading the room and adjusting their lesson.

To be clear, this isn't about white-collar workers becoming obsolete. It's about every worker rethinking which parts of their job require human judgment and which don't, and what will matter most when AI handles the routine work.

Ume is a great example. Her computer science background is still useful, just in a different way than she was taught. The rigorous thinking that engineering teaches remains invaluable: how to break complex problems into components, think systematically, and understand how pieces connect. The job itself, however, is transforming.

Tomorrow's software engineers will spend less time writing code and more time understanding what code should be written. Less time debugging, more time collaborating to define problems worth solving. Less time optimizing algorithms, more time navigating the ethical implications of what they build.

Paul Cheek is a senior lecturer and the senior advisor for entrepreneurship and AI at MIT.[27] He teaches at a place where more than a quarter of undergraduates are computer science majors and says that the changing reality of work, especially as it pertains to computer scientists, is one that schools and students must confront together.[28]

'The question that I go to is, Are students prepared to react to newfound uncertainty? The fact that they can't get a job, are they prepared to react to that? Can they react in an instant like an entrepreneur?'

While Paul believes entrepreneurial thinking is going to become the key to succeeding in tomorrow's economy, he knows the word 'entrepreneur' feels inaccessible to most, especially those outside of the tech sector.

'Entrepreneurship is about more than just starting companies,' he says. 'I believe that the news and the media do a disservice to entrepreneurship in many ways because they set the expectation that those who pursue entrepreneurship are starting companies. And then they go out to raise massive rounds of funding. But the reality is that entrepreneurship is about so much more than that. It's about creating more than is reasonable with the resources we have control of.'

That's it: creating more than is reasonable with the resources we have control of. It's innovating a little, making a change, and stepping off the efficiency treadmill to create something new. Not necessarily a company, but maybe a process or a project. Even just a single improvement.

'The question is not, Are you this stereotypical entrepreneur? The question is, Are you human? Because if you're human, you have this natural inclination to try to create value from nothing.'

Paul demonstrates this when speaking to audiences: 'I'll ask for a volunteer. And I'll have them come up onstage and I'll say, Are you an entrepreneur? And they might say no, and I'll be like, Not yet.'

Then, he asks them to 'think about the most messed up thing that you saw in the world around you' last week. They'll mention a problem from a flight or restaurant. 'I'll say, Okay, how might you fix that?' Suddenly they're generating solutions. 'That is entrepreneurial,' he says with a smile.

'A nurse in a hospital who can figure out some way to increase patient outcomes by manipulating some process or some care initiative or some communication between different medical professionals all of a sudden, if they can do that and have an impact in society simply by doing that, that is entrepreneurial.'

This shift toward entrepreneurial thinking is starting to happen in every field. The people figuring it out aren't racing to automate everything; they're being deliberate about when and how they engage with AI.

The collar system sorted us by what we did. The next era will sort us by how well we can use this new technology to help us get better at the work that only we, as humans, can do. Being more entrepreneurial is a great place to start.

AI as a Colleague, Not a Crutch

Neil Pretty is a straight shooter in his early forties who has built a successful consulting firm, Aristotle Performance, that helps leaders build high-performing teams.[29]

Let It Go

In 2019, a friend showed him a way to use AI to help him learn about potential consulting clients and tailor his sales pitch to them and their interests. Fairly quickly, he saw the perils of overly relying on AI.

'I found it personally distracting,' he says. 'I was too focused on being *it* rather than being *me*, and the result was inauthenticity, and people could smell it a mile away ... What I learned was that AI could do a lot of what I did, but it wouldn't replace me as a person.'

This revelation doesn't mean that Neil doesn't use AI. Far from it. He's just intentional about what he uses it for. He draws on the wealth of information AI can offer, the way you might ask a colleague over coffee for their perspective. After he's consulted AI, he asks himself, How am I going to shape my work based on this new information? He still trusts that he knows how to be himself and serve his clients best. He prioritizes and prizes his human capabilities.

Recently, he was planning a training session, and instead of reaching out to one of his peers, he turned to AI.

'I said, This is what I want to accomplish. This is what I'm thinking. What might you add to this?' Neil says. 'And then I said, What about from the perspective of an organizational development professional, or the perspective of a CEO, or the perspective of this thought leader, or that thought leader? Now, all of a sudden, it can become a source of a lot more perspectives in an instant than my own biased perspective, or than the biased perspectives of one or two individuals whom I would have had to set meetings with, paid ... It eliminated all of that.

OPEN TO WORK

'I have this wonderful exchange that triggered all kinds of new thinking for me,' Neil continues. 'And then I went back to the drawing board and said, Okay, knowing what I know now, how am I going to change my session? And I adapted the session, and the whole process probably took two hours to do what even a couple of years ago would have taken maybe a week.'

What AI did for Neil was trigger new thinking *for him to do*. It didn't do that thinking for him. Neil's approach illustrates the crucial difference between using AI as a tool and using it as a replacement. He treats AI like a colleague who is always there, who never gets tired of questions and can answer them quickly on his schedule, but Neil never forgets that he's the one leading the conversation.

There's an important lesson here. We should all be using AI but we have to be mindful not to misuse it or overuse it, especially in ways that will hamper our own ability to be critical thinkers or creative minds.

The distinction matters. A recent study from MIT found that people who relied solely on AI for writing tasks showed weakened neural connectivity and struggled to accurately quote their own work afterward.[30]

It turns out, when we outsource our thinking entirely to AI, we don't just get worse outcomes; we actually degrade our own ability to think critically. Researchers call that 'cognitive debt.'

Paul from MIT is adamant on this point. 'You can use AI,' he says, 'but there's also an overuse of AI … that sets you back. It doesn't push society forward.'[31]

Let It Go

He notes that, as with the advent of all new technologies, 'people get excited and they get distracted by the shiny object. The reality is that the most successful AI-driven entrepreneurs are those who will integrate the first principles of entrepreneurship with the AI tools.

'Most people are going straight to the AI tools and overlooking most of the first principles: going out and talking to customers, getting to know their customers, defining their customers, figuring out what the burning pain points they have are, translating that into a value proposition, creating a use case and a high-level product specification to solve that need,' he adds. 'And instead they're saying, Let me just jump in and build the whole product because I can. And that, I think, is extremely dangerous because then we wind up building a bunch of products that nobody really wants.'

Letting Go

So, since the dawn of the industrial age, we've valued efficiency above all else, sorted ourselves into collars, and assumed that most of the people at the top of the stacking system had escaped the efficiency work. They hadn't. And now AI is here, coming for that efficiency work that we've all been told to practice hardest. That could be terrifying. Or it could be liberating.

Take Taj English, a twenty-something from Queens.[32] At thirteen, Taj was already building websites in his bedroom with a computer his father bought him. When Taj asked his mother for the money to buy a 'domain name,' she didn't know what that was. She gave him the money anyway.

Taj loves to learn, but traditional schooling was not a good fit for him. He opted for a coding bootcamp instead of college and graduated from General Assembly in 2017. For a while, he was living his dream: writing code for startups, teaching others at General Assembly, building his own apps. Like thousands of other developers, his value was measured by how efficiently he could translate ideas into code, how quickly he could debug systems, and how reliably he could deliver more features faster.

Then came 2023. AI tools like GitHub Copilot and Cursor were suddenly doing much of what Taj had spent years learning, and doing it faster, more accurately, and with fewer bugs. 'The buzz around it made it feel like it was gonna take jobs,' he admits.

But Taj understood something critical that the efficiency-driven economy had suggested he ignore. His best startup idea hadn't come from his coding skills or those technical abilities everyone said were most valuable. Instead, it had come from his weekly trips to the barbershop, watching people wait in long lines, seeing friends ask for stylist recommendations on Facebook. It came from his lived experience, his cultural understanding, his ability to spot problems that others couldn't see.

AI doesn't go to the barbershop. AI didn't grow up knowing what the barbershop means in some communities. But Taj did. In his Caribbean culture, the barbershop isn't just where you get a haircut. It's home. It's community. It's where business gets done and stories get told. As a result, you don't find your barber through a Google search. You find them through word of mouth, through asking, 'Who cuts your hair?'

This deep cultural knowledge shaped every aspect of ListedB, the platform Taj built. It's not just another booking app that anyone else could or would build. ListedB is designed around how Taj's community actually works. Barbers can post their services and manage schedules, yes, but more importantly, clients can share their favorite stylists with friends, recreating digitally what happens naturally in their neighborhood. The platform reflects the truth Taj lived: that in his community, the barbershop is where reputations are built and one satisfied customer leads to three more.

That kind of insight, which was born from relationships, observation, and cultural immersion, was something no algorithm could generate. AI could write the code, but only Taj could recognize what needed to be built and why. The technical skill just made his culturally rooted vision a reality.

Rather than competing with AI at the efficiency game he'd been taught to play, Taj made it his 'junior co-worker.' Now he uses AI to handle the repetitive, mechanical, time-consuming coding work that keeps his business humming while he focuses on what only he can do: create solutions for real problems he understands from lived experience.

Over time, Taj has gone from being a highly efficient coder to being an entrepreneur who uses AI to grow his business faster than ever before. He's scaling his startup by using AI to do what once required a full team, freeing him to focus entirely on the creative and strategic work that actually creates value.

OPEN TO WORK

Taj isn't alone in how he's using AI. Microsoft and LinkedIn's 2024 research confirms the pattern: Of the workers who use AI several times per week, 92 percent say it boosts their creativity and 93 percent say it helps them focus on the most important work.[33]

Again, the future of work isn't about humans versus AI. It's about humans using AI to finally be free to do work that matters: work that draws on our capacity to create solutions to problems other humans actually have. It's about human intelligence being served by artificial intelligence so we can finally focus on what only we can do: innovate.

To get to that new way of work, we have to let go of the more, better, faster mindset. Then we can get ready to do work that uses our full capacity and recognizes the unique capabilities of humans. A lot of us seemed to have forgotten exactly what those are. The next chapter offers a reminder.

The Bottom Line

1. **We're trapped on the efficiency treadmill.** For centuries, we've designed work around industrial efficiency, engineering much of human potential out of jobs and turning people into predictable parts of a productivity machine. AI seems set to unravel all that.

Let It Go

2. **AI remixes; humans create.** AI excels at remixing what already exists, but it can't invent something truly new. Use it to handle routine tasks and expand your perspective, but don't let it do your thinking for you.

3. **Let go of more, better, faster.** AI can handle the efficiency work. Let it. That frees us to do what no algorithm can: create solutions that have never existed before.

CHAPTER 3

The Humans Are Coming

The human brain is a three-pound organ that consumes less energy than a typical lightbulb but somehow generates consciousness, conscience, and the capacity for everything from love to faith.[1] It houses billions of neurons firing at incredibly high speeds in patterns so intricate they remain the most sophisticated network in the known universe.[2]

For centuries, scientists have marveled at the brain's complexity but have also struggled mightily to fully understand it, given the limitations of their tools and methods. In fact, until fairly recently, we generally assumed the brain was static. We thought that once you reached early adulthood, your brain was done developing, and whatever cognitive abilities you had then were all you'd ever get.

That assumption began to crack in the late twentieth century. Researchers started to see hints that the brain might not be so fixed after all and that, in some cases, it could even adapt based on new experiences. And then, in the mid-1990s, an Irish neuroscientist named Eleanor Maguire asked a question that would upend everything.

Watching TV one night, Eleanor happened upon a movie about the grueling tests that London cab drivers have to pass, tests that require spending years memorizing thousands of streets and landmarks. 'I am absolutely appalling at finding my way around,' Eleanor said in an interview with *The Daily Telegraph*.[3] 'I wondered, How are some people so bloody good and I am so terrible?'

As a neuroscientist with access to brain imaging technology, she had a way to find out. She recruited a group of London taxi drivers and scanned their brains. What she found was incredible: A cab driver's posterior hippocampus, which is the brain's memory center, was significantly larger than average.[4] Even more telling, the longer someone had been driving, the larger it was. It turns out, the human brain could grow and strengthen like a muscle.

Around the same time, the cognitive psychologist Anders Ericsson was questioning another long-held belief: that extraordinary talent was innate.[5]

For centuries, Wolfgang Amadeus Mozart's talent was considered so remarkable that it was best understood as divine genius. Thought to have perfect pitch from a very young age, composing by five, performing for European royalty at six, his was a once in forever kind of genius.

When Anders examined Mozart's story more closely, though, a different picture emerged. Mozart's father, Leopold, was a talented musician himself and had begun training with Mozart before he could even speak. By age seven, Mozart had already logged likely as many practice hours as a professional musician. Beyond that, Anders thought about how Mozart grew up in a home saturated with music, where his father composed, his sister was a gifted keyboard player, and music-making was woven into daily life.[6]

What if the 'divine gift' was instead the result of perhaps the most sophisticated early childhood music education program of the eighteenth century?

To push that idea further, Anders drew on the research of Japanese psychologist Ayako Sakakibara, who found that preschool children could reliably develop perfect pitch through systematic early training.[7] The window was narrow and the training had to be precise, but the capability wasn't mystical. It was neurological. And it was trainable.

In 2016, Anders published the book *Peak: Secrets from the New Science of Expertise*, where he distilled decades of research into a simple and powerful idea: Excellence is not simply born but built through what he called 'deliberate practice': focused, feedback-driven effort that is designed to consistently stretch one's abilities beyond comfort.[8]

Peak inspired everyone from educators to executives to rethink how mastery develops, and was part of a growing wave of research revealing the brain's remarkable plasticity. The limits we once saw as fixed have turned out to be quite flexible, especially when there is motivation, born of inherent interest and curiosity, to commit to the deliberate practice of new skills.

And yet, while all this was happening, while scientists were gaining an expanding view of the human brain and how it can grow and adapt in extraordinary ways, the efficiency engine of the economy was solidifying around a narrower definition of human intelligence.

The Century of IQ

In 1905, French psychologists Alfred Binet and Théodore Simon set out to identify schoolchildren who needed special educational support. Their solution was a series of tasks measuring attention, memory, and problem-solving, which became known as the Binet–Simon test.[9]

The test wasn't designed to measure the full spectrum of human intelligence. It was designed to measure the specific cognitive abilities that would help children succeed in an education system that had become anchored around the same efficiency principles that had transformed factories. Students needed to process information quickly, follow standardized procedures accurately, and demonstrate measurable improvement in prescribed time frames.

Binet himself warned that his creation should not be misunderstood as a full measure of intelligence.[10] He understood that intelligence was too complex and multifaceted to capture in a single score, emphasizing that the test was designed to help children by identifying those needing additional support, not to rigidly sort or rank them based on inherent capabilities.

The cultural and technological demands of the industrial age had other plans.

The Humans Are Coming

The Binet–Simon test quickly gained attention in the international psychology community, and within a few years it had made its way to the United States. Researchers here did more than translate the test. They revised it, expanded its range to include adults, and standardized scoring. This happened just before the United States entered World War I in April 1917.

When America entered the war, the army faced the urgent and enormous task of sorting approximately 1.7 million recruits into suitable roles within months.[11] Out of necessity, it quickly adapted the test, assigning scores that influenced whether a recruit would serve as an officer, in support roles, or in the infantry. The test could also determine whether a recruit should be dismissed from the military altogether. It was considered the first mass application of intelligence testing in human history.

Over time, the idea of IQ (intelligence quotient) took off, and we landed on an assertion that human intelligence was mainly about solving puzzles quickly and memorizing facts.

The test became what Binet feared: a tool for measuring human worth by how well minds could serve the demands of a system that valued speed over depth, standardization over creativity, and measurable output over unmeasurable insight. The test both revealed and reinforced what we valued most at the turn of the century, ensuring this narrow definition of human intelligence would dominate assessment for the next hundred years.

In the decades that followed, this definition of intelligence had become cultural common sense. We divided human capability into hard and soft skills, a distinction that solidified further as we entered the knowledge economy, where technical and analytic abilities were prized above all else. Creativity felt somehow lesser than calculus. Compassion was secondary to computation.

Between 2018 and 2023, undergraduate computer science enrollments surged[12] while humanities programs declined.[13] Poetry didn't suddenly become less valuable or philosophy less relevant. We'd simply built an economy that rewarded measurable, technical skills above everything else.

All the while, it turns out, we were also building machines that could do those technical tasks themselves. And what we didn't see coming across all those decades was that once those machines could handle the work we'd trained humans to do, all those soft skills we'd dismissed as less than necessary would suddenly become among the most valuable things we could do as humans.

The Mad Scientist

Vivienne Ming[14] calls herself a 'professional mad scientist' on LinkedIn, and she means it. A neuroscientist turned AI entrepreneur, she delivers most observations with a tongue-in-cheek tone. She's funny, unable to resist a joke. (One of her gripes with AI chatbots? 'The sense of humor of all these things is terrible.') But this irreverent scientist's path to becoming a leading AI researcher was not without profound difficulty.

The Humans Are Coming

'I was supposed to win a Nobel Prize,' Vivienne says of the pressure she experienced during her childhood. Her father, a brilliant man who went from being a poor farmer's son to a doctor, had always wondered if he could have won that prize himself. That expectation eventually fell to Vivienne. 'When you're eleven and you realize for the first time that you're not the smartest person on the planet, maybe not even the smartest person in the room that you're in, that is not a great moment.'

Vivienne suffered from depression as an adolescent and spent a number of years in her twenties homeless as a result of a severe mental health crisis.

In her lowest moments, it was a memory of her father that broke through. 'The thing I took to move me forward was a line from my father. It was: Live a life of substance … I said, I'm going to live a life that makes other people's lives better.'[15]

It took Vivienne some time to get back on her feet. She got a job in a convenience store, then became a manager of a convenience store, and worked her way back onto stable footing.

She ultimately went back to school. She swiftly completed her entire undergraduate degree, earned advanced degrees, became a renowned neuroscientist, and eventually became the chief scientist at a company where she analyzed millions of careers to understand what actually predicts success.

What she discovered challenges much of what we think about achievement. When her team analyzed software developers, they found that resilience, defined by Vivienne's team as the ability to bounce back from stress, was one of the best predictors of coding quality among software engineers. It was better even than a bachelor's degree in computer science from Stanford. Those supposedly 'soft' skills, the ones AI can never replicate, mattered more than a prestigious credential.

Vivienne cites more of her research to back this up. She and her wife, Norma Chang, an education professor, did a study of sixty thousand university students who were enrolled in both undergraduate and graduate courses. To pass these classes, the students were required to regularly post on a public discussion board, posing questions or making comments about the material they were learning.

Vivienne and her wife found that the students essentially fell into two groups. One group regurgitated the material they had been taught in the course in their own words. They were correct, but they weren't really advancing their thinking. The other group posted comments that were 'regularly wrong.' However, these students were 'dramatically more likely to take an idea and explore, though it meant they were publicly wrong on a regular basis.' Unlike the first group, they weren't downloading information in a machinelike way. They were testing that information and trying to actually apply it to novel situations in novel ways.

Vivienne notes that this finding also holds up for people who have extraordinary careers, as she learned through her research. Individuals who achieve at a high level, she says, are 'willing to be wrong in front of other people for the privilege of learning what's right.'

Humans are exceptionally resilient. We are willing and able to fail and bounce back, and that is a big part of what makes us successful. AI isn't resilient in the way we are. It doesn't have to be.

'It doesn't have to overcome failure and move forward. You tell it it's wrong and to do it over again. It does it over again. And again,' Vivienne says. When it does that work, AI is learning, of course, but it's learning how to be *right* to meet the needs of the person prompting it. To give the expected, correct answer. It can't 'take an idea and explore,' in the same ways we humans can. And, more importantly, it can't learn resilience. It can't learn the emotional part of thinking deeply. It can't learn the courage needed to fail and recover from that failure.

So when we spend all that time thinking about all the ways AI is extraordinary in the media, in the corporate world, everywhere, let's not skip over the most extraordinary thing of all. How we came up with AI in the first place. The human brain.

We asked Vivienne whether all this focus on AI means we're underselling the human brain. She laughed. 'Oh, God, yes.'

The 5Cs: Our Edge, Reclaimed

Vivienne's research underscores something crucial: The unique capabilities we have as humans, those skills that we haven't been deliberately measuring, are what make us irreplaceable.

In writing this book, we wanted to understand what these capabilities actually are, so we talked to neuroscientists like

Vivienne, organizational psychologists, behavioral economists, and talent leaders, a wide range of experts who think about human capability and work every day.

We landed on five capabilities, focusing on the core inputs that each of us can develop individually and that, in many ways, enable everything else: curiosity, courage, creativity, compassion, and communication. We call them the 5Cs. The 5Cs make us better teammates and sharper thinkers. Together, they're the engine of human innovation.

As we discussed the 5Cs with experts, Vivienne made a really important point. 'These aren't five separate items on a checklist,' she said. 'They feed each other: Curiosity without courage leads to inaction. Creativity without communication remains a private hobby. Compassion gives our work purpose.'[16]

Curiosity

AI can process patterns. Only humans ask, What if we tried something completely different?

In a moment when AI is reshaping every aspect of how we work, curiosity is our most important advantage as humans. Right now, we can harness that curiosity and the openness that comes with it to learn about AI and how it's going to transform our jobs, to understand ourselves and figure out what makes us irreplaceable, and, most importantly, to align our careers with our curiosities. The questions that fascinate

The Humans Are Coming

you, the ones that keep you up at night or make you lose track of time, are going to be critical to finding your competitive edge in the age of AI.

Curiosity isn't just gathering information. It's wondering why things are the way they are and what happens when you push against those assumptions. Every breakthrough in human history started with someone asking a question no one had asked before. The polio vaccine didn't come from analyzing existing treatments, which is what AI would do.[17] It was invented because Jonas Salk and his colleagues wondered if dead viruses could teach the body to fight live ones. He could have been wrong. He took the time to test his idea anyway. Curiosity is what made Wilbur and Orville Wright wonder, If birds can fly, why can't we?

At work, curiosity makes the routine suddenly become about discovery. The doctor who notices that a patient flinches when discussing something happening in their life and probes deeper, uncovering the real source of stress. The electrician who wonders why a circuit keeps tripping and traces it beyond the obvious answers to find a hidden issue that could have caused a fire. The accountant who questions why certain expenses spike every third quarter and uncovers an inefficiency, saving millions.

Vivienne Ming sees curiosity as her superpower. It has fueled not just the research we discussed earlier but also new, big questions. A recent curiosity of hers questioned why we mostly wait until people get sick to help them, and whether we could use AI to prevent illness rather than just diagnose it. That curiosity led to one of her latest projects, a nonprofit, the

Human Trust, where she is using AI to build a model for better predicting health outcomes for individuals.

Courage

AI can calculate risk. Only humans decide what risk is worth taking.

Courage is the willingness to act without complete information and to move forward when the outcome isn't guaranteed. It's choosing to be the test case when everyone else is waiting for proof. Thousands of years ago, Polynesian wayfarers climbed into hollowed-out trees and set sail across the Pacific, navigating using only the stars and their deep knowledge of the sea. They found new islands, inhabited them, and established cultures that still thrive today. Centuries later, the crew of Apollo 13 carried that same spirit into space. To strap yourself to a rocket and aim for the moon, knowing there was a good chance you may not return, was an act of profound courage. They went anyway, seeking a better understanding of the universe for humankind.

At work, courage turns hesitation into action. The developer who proposes switching to a new framework mid-project because it will serve customers better in the long term. The sales manager who tells a major client their request isn't actually what they need, then helps them find the right solution. The designer who champions a complete rebrand when everyone else is comfortable with the status quo. These aren't people being difficult. They're people choosing progress over comfort. And there's no algorithm for doing what's right when it's hard.

Jonetta Gresham, the AI-skeptic-turned-advocate from chapter 1, provides a useful example here.[18] It took real courage for Jonetta to pursue a career in tech after decades of working as a nurse and a health care consultant. She could have kept taking consulting jobs and accepted that this was how her career would go. Instead, she clicked on an ad for Merit America. She applied for the project management program despite having no formal tech background, despite every voice telling her that people don't pivot careers at her age. Jonetta had the courage to build a path to her future instead of camping out in her past.

Creativity

AI can remix what exists. Only humans reimagine what is possible.

Creativity isn't just artistic expression. It's the ability to generate something genuinely new, not just by recombining existing elements, but by imagining possibilities that never existed before.

Steve Jobs didn't invent the computer, phone, or music player. He took the time to imagine how they could become one device. Sara Blakely cut the feet off her pantyhose and created Spanx, building a billion-dollar business by seeing possibilities where others would have seen a wardrobe malfunction.

At work, creativity isn't confined to 'creative' roles. The nurse who designs a comfort kit for anxious patients after noticing what helps them relax. The data analyst who visualizes information in a way that makes invisible patterns suddenly obvious. The teacher who turns her classroom into a mock archaeological dig to teach history. All those people are not just solving problems but creating new ways of responding to situations that others don't see.

When Ume Habiba from chapter 1 came up with the idea of using fashion to teach girls how to code, she creatively solved a problem that only someone with her perspective could. Not enough girls are entering engineering, and Ume knows from firsthand experience how difficult it is to break into coding as a young woman. So she uses analogies that would have spoken to a younger Ume, a girl who loved fashion and tech, imagining not just new solutions, but solutions that will motivate a specific audience of humans. 'Content creation is what AI just simply cannot do for me that I know I can do,' Ume says.[19]

Compassion

AI can simulate concern. Only humans feel it and express it.

We are a species that cares for each other. In fact, archaeological evidence from thousands and thousands of years ago shows humans with severe disabilities lived for years, something that would have been impossible without community care.[20] Compassion is, in many ways, the foundation of civilization. When a doctor holds a dying patient's hand, that touch carries meaning no robotic comfort can match. AI can mimic compassion, but it cannot actually care for another creature, because so much about how the human brain does this remains unknown.[21] Put more simply, we can't program empathy because we don't know precisely how we do it. We just do it.

At work, compassion is what makes us humans at work, not simply employees at work. Compassion transforms transactions into relationships and teams into communities. The manager who notices an employee's performance dropping and discovers they're caring for a sick parent, then quietly arranges flexible hours. The customer service rep who stays on the phone for longer than needed with a confused customer, walking her through each step.

Neil, the consultant we met in chapter 2, has seen small acts of compassion alter team dynamics completely.[22] He stresses the importance of team members building empathy for one another, even when it feels uncomfortable to connect on a human level. He encourages members of the teams he is coaching to take the time to call each other on the phone just to chat, to say, 'Hey, how's it going? I'm going for a walk, do you want to join me? I'd love to hear how you are doing.'

'It's uncomfortable for most people,' Neil says, but he adds that he's 'seen it fundamentally change the dynamics of a team and their capacity to perform and make good decisions.'

'AI can't do that for you,' Neil reminds us. Being compassionate with each other, that's on us. And when we are, work becomes a better, more human place.

Communication

AI can translate language. Only humans can turn language into meaning.

Communication is what binds us as humans across time and place. It's how knowledge breathes and spreads, from ancient scribes preserving wisdom on clay tablets to scientists building on centuries of shared discovery. Words communicated well have the power to change the world. 'I have a dream' mobilized a movement. 'All you need is love' reframed a generation. 'That's one small step for man …' united the world in a single moment of awe. It's no surprise then that communication ranked globally as the No. 1 in-demand skill on LinkedIn in 2024.[23]

At work, communication determines whether ideas wither or rise. The project manager who aligns a team of engineers, designers, and marketers around a shared vision, despite their different vocabularies and incentives. The CEO who turns skeptical investors into long-term backers by convincing them of a future for the business that doesn't exist yet. The sales rep who listens first and then pitches based on the insights gained, matching solutions to actual needs.

Take this book. It's our attempt to communicate a story

that we hope helps everyone understand and manage this moment of big change at work, especially those of you feeling anxious or confused or skeptical.

Writing a book is an intense endeavor and, in many ways, an intensely human endeavor. AI tools were useful for certain things at certain moments, such as giving feedback on the structure of a chapter or a set of examples. But everything that made this book what it is came from conversations that happened between humans. The two of us, sitting face-to-face, pushing our thinking until we finally got to the book we wanted to write. The team behind this book, brainstorming, researching, questioning, debating, all to advance the arguments and storylines. The interviews we did with workers and experts, all bringing their unique experiences and insights into the book as a model for us all.

With every word, we had to think deeply about the human experience of trying to process a moment of big change and how to, hopefully, eventually, give everyone some agency over it. To do that, you need to know humans. You need to be human.

Soft Skills as the New Hard Skills

The term 'soft skills,' which is often used to describe the 5Cs we've just explored, comes from a time when technical skills were seen as the main drivers of success. That was then. This is now. As AI takes on more routine and technical work, the abilities that make us human are becoming more important.

In the years ahead, we believe these so-called 'soft' skills will be some of the hardest and most valuable to build.

Paul Cheek, the entrepreneurship expert at MIT from chapter 2, notes that the 5Cs are 'the fuel for the future of the economy.'[24]

The thinking here isn't new. In the mid-1990s, psychologist Daniel Goleman brought this broader range of human capabilities from the margins to the mainstream with his groundbreaking work on emotional intelligence.[25] He argued that emotional intelligence, our ability to understand and manage emotions, often matters more than IQ in determining life outcomes. Goleman's framework helped legitimize the idea that qualities like self-awareness, empathy, and social skills were essential for leadership and collaboration.

What's different now is that AI is making Goleman's insight impossible to ignore. While machines excel at processing information and technical tasks, they cannot replicate the emotional attunement and human connection at the heart of the 5Cs. The capabilities Goleman championed are becoming not just advantageous but necessary.

Importantly, the 5Cs aren't capabilities you can pick up from a weekend workshop or an online training module. They are core pieces of who we are and how we think as humans, and they develop only through time, connection, and challenge. They require you to wrestle with hard problems, explore unexpected paths, and test novel ideas in real-world settings.

Let's look again at history. The great innovators of the past have always needed what most modern workers lack: the time and training to think slowly and deeply. Leonardo da Vinci was 'allowed to be driven by pure curiosity,' as Walter Isaacson writes in his biography of da Vinci, because he had patrons who protected his time to explore and experiment without the urgency of efficiency.[26]

Albert Einstein attributed his revolutionary insights not to raw intelligence but to sustained curiosity: 'I have no special talents. I am just passionately curious,' he once observed.[27] His theories took years to develop. Can you imagine getting years to refine an idea at work today?

Time to think deeply is essential, but it's actually only half the equation. Innovation also demands partnership with other humans who are thinking deeply. As Isaacson observes, 'Innovation is a team sport. Creativity is a collaborative endeavor.'[28]

Again, let's look at Einstein. He didn't work in isolation. He wrote to friends, tested ideas with colleagues, and workshopped theories in long conversations. In one letter to a friend, Einstein wrote, 'You and I never cease to stand like curious children before the great mystery into which we were born.'[29] Not just 'I,' but 'you and I.' The greatest breakthroughs emerge from curious minds connecting with other curious minds, which only occurs when they have the ability to explore together and to build on each other's ideas.

We celebrate these stories of deep thinking and collaboration, yet our workplaces tell a different story. Even as career advisors have preached that soft skills matter, even as management consultants have sold the idea, compensation structures, promotion decisions, and hiring practices have generally continued to favor technical credentials over human capabilities.

The reason was simple: In an efficiency-driven economy, technical skills delivered the most easily measured productivity gains. You could quantify the value of a faster coder, a more efficient analyst, a quicker decision-maker. As a result, the incentives we've built around work have prevented most of us from having the chance to develop our non-technical capabilities.

This is why AI represents such a profound opportunity. AI can process information at lightning speed, but it cannot experience the slow burn of curiosity, especially as a shared endeavor with others. It can optimize existing solutions efficiently, but it cannot feel the frustration that sparks entirely new approaches. It can simulate conversation, but it cannot create authentic connections where breakthrough ideas emerge because a meaningful relationship has taken root.

With AI, we have technology that can handle efficiency, freeing us to reclaim time for deep thinking and collaboration as well as providing us with the ability to more easily test and build new ideas and products. The level of innovation that could emerge when everyone has access to AI tools and the time and training that human innovation requires could outstrip anything we've seen to date.

Paul Cheek explains the leveling effect.

'The most successful entrepreneurs previously have either been trained or educated in entrepreneurship, or are experienced entrepreneurs,' he says. 'They had a huge leg up because their business plans would be significantly better than the rest of the population. But now with AI, you can generate an extremely high-quality, rigorous, comprehensive business plan in an instant.

'Instead of spending a year trying to get [an idea] to work, like you might've had to in the past, you can spend a day or two days or three days,' Paul says. 'Entrepreneurs' most precious resources are time and money. If we can run more experiments with far less time and money, ultimately the success rate for a broader range of the population can go up.'

Paul's message is a powerful one. Once we stop trying to compete with AI on efficiency, we can seize the moment to use AI to build work around what makes us most human. We can lean into our capability to develop new ideas, innovate new solutions, and imagine new possibilities.

The next chapter explores how this can happen at scale. We'll look at why some communities produce breakthrough after breakthrough while others don't, and what becomes possible when AI helps more people from more places become entrepreneurial. Innovation from all, for all.

The Bottom Line

1. **The human brain is our most undervalued asset. AI is about to change that.** We've spent a century measuring intelligence by efficiency metrics when our real advantage lies in capabilities that go beyond that.

OPEN TO WORK

2. **The 5Cs are what make us irreplaceable in the AI age.** Curiosity, courage, creativity, compassion, and communication are the capabilities that make us most human and that are core to our competitive edge as humans at work in the age of AI.

3. **Innovation requires time and training.** The greatest breakthroughs have always emerged from minds given the freedom to explore, fail, and connect with others. As AI handles efficiency, we finally have the chance to reclaim the time and skills that human innovation demands.

CHAPTER 4

The Lost Einsteins

Raj Chetty had been asking the same question for years, and nobody seemed to have an answer. As a rising economist in the mid-'00s, he wanted to understand what really determined opportunity in America, but every dataset he could get his hands on told only fragments of the story. Survey data captured snapshots. University records showed who made it to college, not who missed the chance. Corporate databases revealed who succeeded in business, not whose potential went unrecognized.[1]

The breakthrough eventually came from an unexpected source. A profile of Raj in *The Atlantic* describes how, in 2007, the Internal Revenue Service placed an advertisement looking for researchers who could help reformat electronic files. Most academics would have seen this as tedious data work.[2] Raj saw it differently. Who knows more about Americans' economic outcomes than the IRS? Who else has tracked how much money people actually make over their entire lifetimes? Raj and his collaborators jumped at the chance.

OPEN TO WORK

Once Raj began the work, he realized that this data was even more valuable than he had originally thought. It was, in many ways, the key to constructing a complete map of economic opportunity. Why? In 1987, the IRS started requiring Social Security numbers for every dependent listed on a tax return. That meant he could trace children back to their parents. He could see how much money someone's parents made, *and* how much money they would go on to make. For the first time in American history, he could see how economic opportunity really flowed from one generation to another.

Raj's early findings painted a stark picture. His research revealed that children born in 1940 had a 90 percent chance of earning more than their parents, but for children born forty years later, that chance had fallen to 50 percent, essentially a coin flip. Economic opportunity and the mobility it can provide seemed to be stalling out.

But Raj wasn't finished. As he continued mining this dataset, he turned his attention to a question that strikes at the heart of this book. When we think about how we're going to build an economy based on entrepreneurialism and innovation, we have to consider not just *how* humans innovate but *who* gets to innovate in the first place.

In 2018, Raj and a team of collaborators analyzed the lives of the 1.2 million inventors in America who filed a patent over a period of nearly two decades.[3] They traced each one back to childhood, looking for patterns by first looking at things like test scores from early years in school. The data revealed how stark the divide is between talent and opportunity.

The Lost Einsteins

The researchers found that 'among students with test scores in the top 5% of the distribution, those from high-income families are more than twice as likely to become inventors as those from lower-income families. This result suggests that becoming an inventor in America relies on two traits: having high inventive ability (as proxied for by math test scores early in childhood) *and* being born into a high-income family.'

Overall, children from the wealthiest 1 percent of families were ten times more likely to become inventors than those from lower-income households. Ten times. And the reason wasn't raw ability. It was ultimately about proximity. Living near inventors directly affected a child's likelihood of becoming one.

Move a child from a low-innovation area to a high-innovation area and you increase their chances of inventing meaningfully. The effect is uncannily specific. Kids don't just become inventors; they often become exactly the type of inventor they grow up seeing. 'Among people living in Boston,' Chetty and his co-authors wrote, 'those who grew up in Silicon Valley are especially likely to patent in computers, while those who grew up in Minneapolis – which has many medical device manufacturers – are especially likely to patent in medical devices.'[4]

It turns out you absorb not just the knowledge of those around you when you are growing up but an idea of what is possible for your future. Without seeing people from your background succeed as innovators, the idea that you could be one never forms in your mind.

The research touches on a deeper truth about how human progress itself has always worked.

A Playbook for Success

Just over a decade ago, deep in the caves of Gibraltar, the archaeologist Clive Finlayson and his team made a discovery that challenged one of our most cherished myths. On a rock wall they found eight deliberate grooves etched in a hashtag-like pattern. The marks were thirty-nine thousand years old, likely the work of Neanderthals.[5]

Until then, we had told ourselves a fairly simple story: Neanderthals were strong but unimaginative while we Homo sapiens survived because we had the capacity for creation. We painted caves, made jewelry, and invented. As a result, they endured but we evolved.

Gibraltar showed otherwise. Neanderthals had symbolic thought too, and could potentially make meaning beyond survival. Suddenly, we had to confront the reality that imagination wasn't uniquely ours. Why, then, did we survive when they did not?

There are lots of reasons for that and lots of people better suited to answer that question than we are. But part of the answer does seem to tie back to what anthropologists call 'the ratchet effect,'[6] the way our species has advanced through a process of shared innovation, where each person's ideas build on the discoveries of others and lead to the discoveries of others.

The Lost Einsteins

Where Neanderthal innovations often flickered in isolated groups, our breakthroughs seemed to compound.[7] We invented the mechanisms, from languages to rituals to stories, that allowed ideas to leap across villages, then continents, then centuries. One person's insight became another person's foundation. Each generation and each century built on the past and was built upon in the future.

'Chimps can show other chimps how to hunt termites,' said Christopher Henshilwood, an archaeologist at the University of the Witwatersrand, in an interview with *Scientific American*. 'But they don't improve on it, they don't say, "Let's do it with a different kind of probe" – they just do the same thing over and over.'[8]

Consider one of our 5Cs: communication.

For millennia, humans communicated the tracking of goods with clay tokens, using things like a cone for grain. Then, a few thousand years ago, our ancestors started to develop signs that could convey things people were saying too, not just items or objects. Those signs became words, and those words, which captured more and more complex thought over time, made permanent the ideas that humans were discussing and debating through spoken word. That meant that, over time, our ancestors started learning not just from those around them but from people in other places and from other times.

The printing press took all this to a new level. To see the impact for humankind, watch what happened with just one area of constant interest: astronomy.

Our ancestors had gazed upward and built models of what existed at the outer reaches of our sight, but each generation had to spend most of their time recreating or incrementally refining the observations of the previous generation rather than building on them. And they did that often in isolation of other communities doing the same thing. The Maya crafted detailed almanacs. Chinese astronomers catalogued hundreds of stars by 300 BCE. Islamic scholars preserved and advanced these ideas with empirical methods.[9]

Once the printing press arrived, astronomers didn't have to spend years copying previous observations by hand. In 1543, when Copernicus published his theory that the Earth revolved around the sun, he stood on the shoulders of centuries of observers.[10] He drew on Ptolemy's models, Islamic astronomical tables,[11] and observations from across continents, many of which were increasingly available in print rather than scattered solely in rare manuscripts.[12]

Galileo built on Copernicus's foundation, but he also had something Copernicus lacked: the telescope, invented in the early 1600s and rapidly refined by Galileo himself. With more printed knowledge at hand and this new instrument pointed at the sky, he could find evidence to support Copernicus's theory.

Newton could synthesize both their works because their ideas were increasingly available in print rather than locked away. That foundation, combined with the time and space to think, allowed him to notice something as mundane as an apple falling from a tree and connect it to all that astronomical research.

As Newton himself said, 'If I have seen further, it is by standing upon the shoulders of giants.'[13] On those shoulders he realized that the same force pulling the apple downward is the one that keeps planets in orbit. One universal law governs both: the law of universal gravitation.

Each generation reached higher because they didn't have to rebuild the foundation. That leap from clay tokens to printed books unleashed an explosion of human innovation, not because of the marks themselves, but because we built on them together, across communities and centuries.

Along the way, machines certainly helped us humans do all that. Since the industrial age, however, they have also shifted our focus at work. We started measuring ourselves by their standards, causing us too often to forget what made us distinct.

Now, as AI transforms everything around us, it's time we remember what made us human in the first place. The ratchet effect only turns forward, and it only turns when human hands and human minds, working together across place and time, give it motion. This is not just our history. It's core to the playbook for our success as a species.

Let Everyone Be Amazing

Raj's findings reveal how thoroughly we've failed at this. The patterns in his data show certain communities have been excluded from the arena of innovation. Those historically shut out of elite institutions, who grew up in regions far from tech hubs, with parents who worked with their hands instead of with patents? They show the same capabilities as their wealthier counterparts in early years, but they rarely become inventors.

Raj calls them 'Lost Einsteins,' people who would have delivered significant inventions had the system recognized their potential and supported their rise.[14] The economic waste is staggering. If all communities innovated at the same rate as those with historical access to elite networks, the research suggests America would have four times as many inventors.

And it's not just America. The same pattern appears all over the world.

Researchers from Harvard and the University of Bristol found that Math Olympiad competitors from developing nations, despite matching the scores of their wealthy-country counterparts, produce significantly fewer academic publications later in life.[15] In a separate study, a group of international economists analyzing Finnish military aptitude tests against innovation records found that when teenagers grow up in affluent, highly educated families rather than middle-income ones, their likelihood of creating patented inventions dramatically increases.[16]

Think about how this reality is playing out right now in the world as it is currently. A nurse's aide who is navigating health care's daily failures could be revolutionizing patient care, but never saw anyone from her neighborhood filing patents. A factory worker who instinctively betters workflows could be transforming manufacturing, but saw invention as something for people with degrees, not skills. A teacher in rural America who sees patterns others miss might be advancing AI itself, but felt they had no place in Silicon Valley.

So many people already excel at the 5Cs and the habits of entrepreneurialism because they've had to. When systems aren't built for you, creativity becomes survival. When you're first in your family to navigate professional settings, communication across differences is a daily reality. When you lack connections, courage to put yourself out there is the only way forward.

Yet without exposure to people who've turned those capabilities into recognized innovations, all that potential remains largely untapped. Not just by others but by themselves. 'These people have the talent to be inventors, but they don't imagine that they could be,' explains MIT economist John Van Reenen, a co-author of the Lost Einsteins study.[17]

As Vivienne, the neuroscientist, says, 'Everyone is amazing. It is simply that the vast majority of people will never lead the life that allows them to actually realize that amazing. I don't even like to think of potential. Not they *could* be amazing; they *are* amazing. We have to own the failure of not allowing them to become that person.'[18]

The New Einsteins

There is hope. Tess Posner, a musician and entrepreneur, is working to fix the failure Vivienne describes.[19] Trained as a social worker, Tess has a calm and comforting demeanor. She approaches her mission, however, with relentless tenacity.

As the founding CEO of AI4ALL, Tess has helped thousands of young people access AI education. Her goal is not simply to teach young people how to code, but to help them discover that they have a fundamental role to play in shaping the future of technology.

OPEN TO WORK

Tess's path to becoming an AI champion started in the woods of Massachusetts, where she grew up with a carpenter father and teacher mother. At sixteen, she traveled to El Salvador with Habitat for Humanity to build houses after an earthquake. Seeing three-year-olds whose teeth were rotting due to the lack of basic health care, she experienced what she calls a crystallizing moment: 'Human value, human dignity, and human worth are the core things, but opportunity is not equally distributed based on that.'

That realization led her to study philosophy, then social work. By 2012, she was training people in economically disadvantaged communities from Arkansas to California in basic digital skills.

'We were focusing on communities left out of the tech economy and how technology can help accelerate them and their economic mobility,' she says.

All along, Tess understood something crucial: It wasn't enough to teach people the skills necessary to build the future if they didn't see themselves in the future that was being built. When she interviewed to be the first CEO of AI4ALL in 2016, she saw the chance to intervene at the moment that would define everything else.

'Artificial intelligence isn't just going to shape the future of work,' she realized. 'It's going to shape the future of being human.'

AI4ALL does more than teach students to build AI systems. Through project-based learning, students tackle real problems they see in their communities: early detection of brain tumors, credit card fraud that devastates families living paycheck to paycheck, environmental monitoring in underserved areas. These projects are all problems that these students hope to solve because they viscerally understand them as part of their lived experiences.

'We're telling people how to memorize facts, right? But education is not about that,' Tess insists. 'It's about discovering who you are. It's a transformational experience.' Tess stresses the importance of time, both to do deep thinking and to develop close networks. In AI4ALL's programs, 90 percent of students leave feeling connected to a community, Tess says, which is crucial for students who've been historically excluded from tech spaces.

Tess hopes to ensure that the 'Lost Einsteins' shape the technology that will define all of our futures. As she puts it, 'We have this opportunity to imagine something. We have the opportunity to create and steer it in a particular direction, but people think about technology as destiny. Actually, we are at this inflection point, and we do have the power and the responsibility to shape it.'

Across the Atlantic, Joséphine Goube,[20] a French social entrepreneur in her mid-thirties, is hoping to find 'Lost Einsteins' among a different population: refugee women fleeing hardship in countries like Ukraine, Afghanistan, and Syria. These are women who already have so many capabilities but whose talents remain largely invisible to traditional systems.

Joséphine's nonprofit, Sistech, teaches these women AI literacy, pairs mentees with mentors in tech, and encourages community building among members. Sistech is also creating an AI that can develop comprehensive analyses of its members' skills and suggest a learning path personalized to their backgrounds and professional pasts.

While still in development, the tool does already have a name: Lena. What makes Lena special is that it can help surface the value of life experience. Lena will be able to analyze how a woman's personal experiences have built her 5C capabilities, then suggest tailored courses and career matches based on those strengths.

Joséphine notes a woman might ask Lena about the value of a particular life experience in the job market, or about how to translate past job experience from her home country to similar roles in her host country. Then, Lena will bring up particular skills and say, yeah, these are the organizational and planning competencies that you developed through experience, being a mother of five. Or, with your ten years of experience as a prosecutor in your country, your forensic investigation skills are truly valuable for a local cybersecurity job opening.

Seventy to eighty percent of Sistech's participants find jobs in tech. A true scientist, Joséphine is not satisfied with the fact that the program works. She wants to know why. So she studied it. Her research points to the effectiveness of two interventions: first, training her members in AI tools that help them get past language and cultural barriers, thereby saving them the time and effort of writing emails in a new language when AI can translate complex thoughts from their mother tongues swiftly; and second, the role modeling the women do for each other and the community they build among themselves.

The women, Joséphine says, realize that they are encountering 'the same problems, that it's not *their* problem [alone] …

The Lost Einsteins

They lost confidence, they were like, I'm just not skilled, just not good enough, and then they meet another woman from Iraq, or another woman from Egypt, and they're like, No, it's the same for all of us.'

Teaching Innovation

AI4ALL and Sistech prove what's possible. But reaching millions of 'Lost Einsteins' will require more than exceptional nonprofits. It will require meaningful redesigns to the system that shapes every human from our earliest days: education itself.

That presents a massive challenge. For more than a century, our systems of education have been largely built off the same efficiency principles that shaped the industrial economy, with a focus on faster learning, more content coverage, and better test scores.

What matters now isn't teaching students to outpace machines. It's giving them time to think more deeply than machines ever could.

Diego Arambula, vice president for education transformation at the Carnegie Foundation[21] for the Advancement of Teaching, has spent years studying what schools across America actually want for students. He finds remarkable alignment throughout the country.

'Urban, rural, red state, blue state, doesn't matter,' Diego says. 'People want the same thing for young people.' School vision statements across the country emphasize the same capabilities: collaboration, creativity, critical thinking. The 5Cs show up everywhere, he says.

The challenge is developing these capabilities within a system that remains built for efficiency.

Diego, a former classroom teacher, saw this tension first-hand. When teaching the French Revolution, he'd say to students, 'There are things you need to know: dates, key figures, causes. That's the floor, not the ceiling. Facts matter. Context matters. But when education treats content mastery as the endpoint, [and] when knowing information earns you an A, we've applied efficiency thinking to learning itself.'

The deeper work requires what the focus on efficiency has largely caused us to push aside: time to grapple with complex problems, space to explore questions without predetermined answers, and permission to fail and iterate. That's where distinctly human capabilities develop.

Individual teachers like Diego have been fighting for this approach for years. Now institutions are starting to follow.

College Board is the nonprofit organization that designs and administers the SAT and Advanced Placement (AP) courses and assessments. AP courses are college-level courses offered to high school students in America that allow them to take on more rigorous material and potentially earn college credit. The courses were first introduced in the 1950s but became widespread in the 1990s. For three decades now, taking an AP course, or multiple AP courses, has been a way of signaling rigor in high school. According to College Board, as of 2025, 89 percent of high schools offer AP courses.

The Lost Einsteins

Over the past few years, College Board has been developing a new set of career-focused courses that develop the 5Cs and, importantly, the skills employers say they are looking for. The hope is to meet the needs of the new economy, and expand the reach of the AP and the achievement it signals.

In 2025, College Board launched the series by debuting AP Cybersecurity, AP Networking, and AP Business with Personal Finance.[22]

In the AP Business with Personal Finance course, students become financial analysts and advisors for a mock household, grappling with real questions: How much insurance should they carry? Should they rent or buy? This isn't theoretical learning but applied practice that fosters students' ability to imagine their own futures.

The course also encourages and teaches entrepreneurship as students learn to spot opportunities in the market, think about customer problems and needs, and build products and services to address them. They do this through the hands-on work of developing and creating a business, starting with the initial idea, then moving into market research, hypothesis testing, and prototyping.

By expanding the type of courses they provide, College Board is hoping to make the APs more relevant to more students. To date, even though AP classes are widely available, it's mostly higher-income students who sign up, while lower-income students have not participated at expected levels. The practical value of the new set of courses could help reverse that trend.

Paul Cheek, the leader of MIT's center for entrepreneurship, was involved with the launch of these new courses, partially because he credits his entrepreneurial drive to both his high school job working in a grocery store *and* a high school course, much like the one College Board has designed, on entrepreneurship.[23]

'I was very fortunate to have an entrepreneurship class in my public high school,' Paul says. 'Most of the population does not have that. And I think that's a critical missing link.'

These courses represent a first step away from the industrial model, helping students think entrepreneurially rather than training them to be efficient information processors. By expanding what 'rigor' means beyond traditional academics, these courses are also creating pathways for students who've been held back from demonstrating the fullest extent of their capabilities.

Of course, the big shift here must extend beyond high school. It requires rethinking how we approach higher education as well, especially when it comes to the humanities. Remember the enrollment trends we examined earlier? Computer science majors surged while humanities enrollments shrank as students made rational decisions about career prospects. That calculation is about to shift.

Literature, philosophy, and history have spent centuries helping humans develop versions of the 5Cs through skills like critical analysis, ethical reasoning, cultural understanding, and empathy. Those are all skills we now recognize as crucial in the AI era. What's missing is the institutional bridge to employers.

Universities have navigated such transitions before. For centuries, mathematicians explored problems in a mostly abstract way. When the industrial age created new demands at work, those theories suddenly became essential. Universities adapted. New forms of science and engineering degrees emerged to translate abstract mathematics into employable skills. Similarly, the humanities will need new structures and degrees to make them essential in the AI age.

Some institutions are already experimenting with cross-disciplinary programs that blend the humanities with technical fields. The University of Illinois Urbana-Champaign offers a Computer Science and Philosophy major that teaches students how to build extraordinary computing innovations while navigating their ethical implications.[24] The Department of Digital Humanities at King's College London is a world-leading center that explores how new technologies intersect with culture, society, and the humanities.[25] The work there combines critical theory and practical skills to study and shape the impact of the digital on human life.

Other institutions are creating clearer pathways from humanities degrees to jobs. In 2017, the University of Arizona created the Department of Public and Applied Humanities.[26] The program shows students how to apply some of the trademarks of the humanities, like curiosity and storytelling, to personally meaningful real-world problems. Career-readiness courses demonstrate how their skills translate to the job market. In a similar vein, Oregon State University offers an online BA/BS in applied humanities for adult learners, recognizing that humanities skills are essential for today's job market, with emphasis on communication and interpersonal development.[27]

OPEN TO WORK

These programs are all united by an important goal: making the connection between the humanities and economic value clear to students, parents, and employers.

The Innovation Explosion

Talent is evenly distributed but opportunity is not. That's been true across human history. What's also been true is that progress for humanity has largely depended on two things: how widely knowledge could spread and how easily individuals could do something with that knowledge.

The printing press spread knowledge to the extent that anyone who could get a book and knew how to read could learn what scholars knew. It transformed who could access ideas, turning a handful of learned elites into engaged communities and societies. You still needed other resources, however, like capital, connections, and technical expertise, to turn what you learned into something real.

The internet took this further. It opened up not just access to knowledge but also access to other people, such that anyone could see what the world knew and, more easily than ever before, find others working on the same pursuits or problems.

Even with that advance, the barriers to building something new remained high. You could do your research and find partners to connect with, but the execution of innovation, especially at scale, required funding and technical skills most people didn't have or couldn't get.

AI changes this dynamic completely.

The Lost Einsteins

First, AI personalizes in ways no tool could before. It learns from you, adapts to you, and improves with you. The printing press gave everyone the same book. The internet gave everyone pretty much the same search results. AI gives everyone a tool that becomes theirs, understanding their context, their constraints, and their goals, all while getting better at helping them the more they use it.

Second, AI democratizes access to expertise. You no longer need years of training to access world-class knowledge in a field. A farmer can use AI to apply soil science insights to the specific conditions they are facing. A mechanic can run engineering simulations that once required advanced degrees and expensive software. The expertise gap, which has always determined who could attempt innovation and who could not, is shrinking before our eyes.

Third, and perhaps most importantly, AI democratizes execution itself: the ability to test, prototype, and iterate. The social worker can now build and test an app to solve transportation gaps in his community. The teacher can create and refine support tools. The factory worker can model workflow improvements and see them visualized before implementation. You don't need venture capital to try your idea anymore. You don't need a team of engineers from elite institutions. You simply need the insight only you have and the will to act on it.

Jensen Huang, Nvidia's CEO, recently said he doesn't think AI will eliminate human jobs unless 'the world runs out of ideas.'[28] We may actually be headed for the opposite: an explosion of ideas from people and places that have been blocked out of the arena of innovation.

OPEN TO WORK

Across human history, so many good ideas were locked in minds that lacked the means to act. People too busy surviving to innovate, too exhausted from efficiency work to imagine something new, too situated in traditional paths to build new ones. Every major challenge we face in our time, from climate change to health care, might have solutions waiting in those minds. And in our time, the means to act on those ideas could soon be everywhere too.

At this point in the book, we hope you understand what we're leaving behind as AI transforms work: a centuries-old focus on efficiency that has led us too often to undervalue our deeper capabilities as humans. In the next section, we'll look at how this transformation is going to reshape every level of work: your job, your career, your company, and even the economy itself.

The Bottom Line

1. **Millions of Lost Einsteins have been locked out of innovating.** Zip codes predict innovation better than talent does because ability isn't enough. You need to see people who are like you succeed. Without role models, brilliance can stay buried.

2. **Education needs to shift focus from what machines do well to what humans do uniquely.** Students can learn and hone entrepreneurialism and the 5Cs through programs like AI4ALL and the new AP classes. When education connects to real problems and human solutions to those problems, students learn better.

3. **An innovation explosion is within reach.** For the first time, anyone with an idea could soon be able to build, test, and scale solutions. If that happens, breakthrough innovations could soon emerge from all over.

PART II
WHAT'S CHANGING

CHAPTER 5

Jobs Are Tasks, Not Titles

Bette Nesmith Graham was never supposed to be a secretary. A high school dropout who'd earned her GED in night school, she dreamed of being an artist.[1] In the early 1950s, she was a single mother living in Dallas, and she needed steady work to support her young son, Michael. So she typed, slowly and imperfectly, as an executive secretary for the chairman of Texas Bank and Trust.

Then came technology that was meant to make everything easier: electric typewriters. IBM promised these machines would transform office work. They offered faster typing and less physical effort, and were seen as the future of efficiency. Banks and corporations rushed to modernize, replacing their manual typewriters with these technological marvels.

When Texas Bank and Trust made the switch, Bette's struggles multiplied. She was already considered a slow typist, prone to errors. Now the new machines made things worse. Their sensitive keyboards responded to the lightest touch, which was a blessing for fast typists but a curse for careful ones. The carbon-film ribbons left impressions so dark and permanent that corrections were impossible. One mistake meant retyping the entire page.

While other secretaries felt frustration at the need to start over each time they made a mistake, Bette saw something different. As an aspiring artist, she had held many jobs to make ends meet, including painting letters on bank windows. She knew that sign painters never started over; instead, they painted over their mistakes.

One night, she pulled out her kitchen blender and whipped up some tempera water-based paint, tinting it to match the bank's stationery. The next day, she brought a small bottle and watercolor brush to work. Her boss never noticed the painted-over corrections. The other secretaries sure did.

Soon Bette was mixing batches at home, filling bottles labeled 'Mistake Out' for the growing number of secretaries who wanted her magic solution. By 1956, she'd officially started the Mistake Out Company, employing Michael and his friends to help with production.

The balancing act of her day job and side job couldn't last. Orders grew, especially after a trade magazine featured the product and General Electric placed a major order. Bette became increasingly distracted at her day job. Her boss at the bank finally fired her for neglecting her secretarial duties.

Free to focus on her invention full time, Bette refined the formula, renamed it Liquid Paper, and built it into a million-dollar business. By 1979, Gillette bought the company from Bette for $47.5 million, which is equivalent to over $200 million today.[2] Along the way, she modernized not just error correction but company culture, establishing childcare for employees and two foundations to help women in need.

Bette's story offers us an important lesson as we approach this moment of big change.

Bette didn't succeed by becoming a better typist. The technological advancement actually made her worse at her job, at least as that job had been defined for her. She succeeded because she recognized that her real job wasn't typing, it was producing perfect documents. When technology made that harder for her, she didn't protect her old way of working. Instead, she drew on knowledge others would have considered irrelevant: artistic savvy and technical insights from a job she'd only taken because she was a struggling single mother.

Your Job Is Not Your Title

When someone asks, 'What do you do?' you probably respond with your title. 'I'm a marketer.' 'I'm an engineer.' 'I'm a barista.' 'I'm a CEO.' It's how we've been taught to think about work: as fixed roles with fixed boundaries.

And, honestly, it makes sense. For decades, that's exactly how organizations have seen you and, as a result, how you have likely seen yourself. Your title determines your pay grade, your place in the hierarchy, and your career path. Performance reviews measure you against standardized role descriptions. This is how an associate, a manager, a director, a vice president all are expected to perform. The entire architecture of work, from your first job to your last job, has been organized around these standards.

We've internalized all this so deeply that, for many, our titles became our identities. 'I *am* an accountant,' not 'I do accounting.' Again, it makes sense. The systems of work trained us to see ourselves this way. That's how advancement works. That's how value is measured. That's how we understand our place in the professional world.

AI doesn't care about your title. It doesn't respect the boundaries of your job description. It comes for tasks, one by one, upending roles from the inside out. Suddenly defining yourself by a title that means less each day isn't just limiting. It's kind of dangerous.

Think about it. Your title might say 'financial analyst,' but what do you actually do? You gather data from multiple sources. Spot patterns others miss. Translate numbers into stories executives can understand. Calm nervous stakeholders. Mentor junior team members. Navigate office politics to get buy-in.

Which task defines you? All of them. None of them. That's the point.

For too long, many of us have let a title be our professional story. But you're not just a financial analyst, a plumber, or a nurse practitioner. You're not *just* anything. You're a collection of distinctly human capabilities, contributions, and potential that no title captures.

Letting go of a title as the fullest description of what you do may be intimidating, especially if doing so goes against all you've been told to focus on to date. But reimagining your job through the lens of tasks, through the actual work you do rather than the title you have, can be liberating. It can give you greater ownership and control over your professional story. And there's research that shows why this task-based view of work matters so much.

The University of Pennsylvania professor Adam Grant[3] and his colleagues discovered something interesting while studying organizations like the Make-a-Wish Foundation. Employees who created 'self-reflective' titles, ones that captured how they saw what they did rather than their formal position, experienced less burnout and more engagement. The reason is that they were able to feel their whole selves in their professional lives. They could name and curate those tasks in a way that felt genuine to them.

Adam's work ties to research done by Amy Wrzesniewski and Jane Dutton, who, years earlier, coined the term 'job crafting.'[4] The two found that when employees are able to craft their jobs so that they align with their strengths, interests, and values, it leads to higher engagement, satisfaction, and resilience. Job crafting can be done in our minds, tying the purpose of our job to impacts we find personally important, or it can be done in real life, changing the way we craft our jobs by adding in tasks and responsibilities that allow us to feel more connected and impactful at work.

As we enter the age of AI, this task-based view is going to become essential to managing the change as it unfolds. But which tasks are changing first and how should you respond?

And how do you start preparing more generally for the way AI will shift your work? With the same mental model Bette used when she separated mechanical typing from human judgment.

Bette knew the typewriter could produce neat letters quickly, but it couldn't spot spelling errors. It could make documents look professional but not perfect. Her job was to use the machine to do both. She worked her way through some big questions. What is the purpose of my job? How does technology help me and how does it hinder me? Then, she went even deeper, even if she wasn't doing it with the same intentionality we're asking of you. What part of my job does the machine do on its own? What part do the machine and I do together? What can only I do?

This same lens shows any worker, in any role or industry, exactly where AI creates risk and where it creates opportunity. It's time to sort your work into buckets.

The Three-Bucket Framework

This framework will help you see exactly where AI will impact your work and where your unique human advantage lies.

Grab a piece of paper. Write down the top dozen tasks that take up most of your time at work. Not your job title or job description. These are the actual things you do day to day. Now sort them into three buckets:

Bucket 1: Tasks AI Can Do Alone

These are the routine, predictable tasks that follow clear rules and work with structured data. They require accuracy and consistency more than judgment or creativity. Think of them as the tasks where being human adds no big, special value, where perfect execution matters more than personal touch.

Common examples include generating standard reports from data, checking for errors against established criteria, answering frequently asked questions, searching databases, and any task that follows an 'if this, then that' pattern.

Ask yourself: Could someone else do this task exactly the same way I do? Does it have clear right and wrong answers? Would a perfect machine do it better? If yes, it belongs in Bucket 1.

For those of you having difficulty getting started with this, you can take it as an opportunity to experiment with AI. Feed an AI tool a list of your tasks and ask, 'What of this can you do?'

Bucket 2: Tasks You'll Do with AI

These tasks blend technological capability with human capability. They require both data processing and contextual understanding, both efficiency and empathy, both pattern recognition and strategic thinking. Here, AI amplifies your capabilities but can't replace your experience, intuition, or understanding of nuance.

In practice, this looks like using AI to analyze data and find patterns, but knowing that AI can't replace your ability to determine which of those patterns actually matter to your specific business. It's having AI draft content that's technically correct, then using your personal experience to make it emotionally resonant. It's using AI to provide you helpful background for customer interactions, but using your human intuition to read between the lines for what's not being said. The technology handles the basics of the task; we humans make the task meaningful.

Success in this bucket requires AI literacy: not just knowing how to use AI tools to do your job better, but understanding which tools to use for which tasks. With new AI capabilities emerging constantly, and AI agents on the horizon that can handle entire workflows, knowing how to evaluate and select the right tool for the moment becomes a skill in itself. The landscape is expanding rapidly, and navigating it effectively is part of the work.

Ask yourself, Does this task require understanding context that's not in the data? Do I need to apply judgment based on experience? Would the best outcome come from combining AI's capabilities with human insight? If yes, it belongs in Bucket 2.

Bucket 3: Tasks That Remain Uniquely Human

These are the irreducibly human tasks involving those 5Cs we discussed earlier. Tasks that involve emotional intelligence, creative problem-solving, ethical judgment, and complex relationship building. They emerge from the unpredictable nature of human interaction and can't be reduced to patterns or rules. They're about reading unspoken dynamics, building trust, navigating ambiguity, and creating something genuinely new. Maybe even, like Bette, an entirely new product and business.

Think about calming a nervous client by sensing their unspoken fears. Or mediating between colleagues whose conflict is upending the team. Or knowing when to break from standard procedure because the situation is different. These tasks require presence, intuition, and the full complexity of human understanding.

Ask yourself, Does this require reading emotions or building trust? Does it involve ethical judgment or navigating competing interests? Would a human touch make the crucial difference? If yes, it belongs in Bucket 3.

The Assessment

Now look at your three buckets. Be honest. What percentage of your time goes to each?

The math here tells you a lot about your vulnerability and your opportunity.

If more than half of your tasks fall into Bucket 1, you're in the red zone. Not tomorrow, today. Your job is already being upended. These routine, rule-based tasks are AI's sweet spot. The technology exists. The economic incentive is clear. The only question is timing.

If around half are in Bucket 1, you're in the yellow zone. You have time, but not much. The clock is ticking on developing your Bucket 2 and 3 capabilities. You're like a frog in slowly heating water, comfortable enough today that you might miss the moment when change becomes urgent.

If less than half are in Bucket 1, you're in the green zone, for now. But don't celebrate yet. That percentage is growing for everyone as AI capabilities expand.

Now here's what that breakdown doesn't tell you at first glance: Vulnerability isn't just about how many Bucket 1 tasks you have. It's about the relationship between all three buckets.

If your Bucket 2 is nearly empty, you're missing the biggest opportunity in this new era for work. These hybrid tasks, where human judgment meets machine capability, are where the new work happens. If you're not actively building this bucket, you're leaving an advantage you can get with AI untapped. You should be experimenting with AI tools weekly, if not daily, finding ways to amplify your human capabilities, not replace them.

Research from Microsoft and LinkedIn found that workers using AI say it helps them save time (90 percent), focus on their most important work (85 percent), be more creative (84 percent), and enjoy their work more (83 percent).[5] Our data also shows that employees who build AI skills are more likely to develop key people skills too. That makes sense: Working well with AI requires constant translation between human problems and technical solutions, which naturally strengthens communication, collaboration, and critical thinking.

If your Bucket 3 is less than half, your current job is limiting your ability to hone the uniquely human skills that will help create lasting career security. Your irreplaceable capability to build trust, navigate ambiguity, and genuinely innovate is your protection against disruption. Despite all the AI hype among business leaders, a 2023 LinkedIn Executive Confidence Index survey found that 92 percent of U.S. executives agree that soft skills are more important than ever. Even more encouraging is that these skills can be developed with intentional practice.

Over time, success is about moving tasks across your buckets. Start deliberately moving tasks from Bucket 1 to Bucket 2 by adding human judgment to routine work. Start using AI tools in Bucket 2 to free up time for more Bucket 3 tasks. And start expanding your Bucket 3 capabilities, because that's where durable value lives.

Think of it as a conveyor belt. Bucket 1 tasks will increasingly disappear as AI gets more advanced. But as they do, new opportunities emerge in Bucket 2, allowing you to use AI to do things that weren't possible before. And as you master Bucket 2, you create space and ideas for deeper Bucket 3 work that no machine can touch.

'The most critical skill here isn't just sorting tasks into buckets, but developing the meta-skill of actively curating them over time,' neuroscientist Vivienne Ming says. 'This is a process of ongoing adaptation for us all, not a onetime exercise.'[6]

Adaptability, the New Competitive Advantage

That brings us to adaptability, which is an essential skill for us all right now. As Paul Cheek from MIT says about computer science majors graduating into the job market, the question isn't whether they can currently find jobs, it's whether they have 'the entrepreneurial mindset and skill [that] would enable them to react to that uncertainty.'[7] In other words, to adapt. To pivot. To see opportunity in the midst of disruption and stay resilient and curious along the way.

Adaptability was one of the top three fastest-growing skills on LinkedIn in 2024, and the World Economic Forum (WEF) notes that 'resilience, flexibility and agility' are among the most essential skills employers will need in the coming years.[8] As we said earlier, even if we're not changing jobs, our jobs are changing on us. How should we manage that? History offers a helpful lesson.

When ATMs arrived in the 1970s, some experts predicted that the job of the bank teller was on its way out. The logic was simple. If a machine could dispense cash, why pay a human to do it? As an article in 1973 in *The New York Times* read, 'To an enthusiastic banker these machines, used today by many people to provide emergency cash, are considered

Jobs Are Tasks, Not Titles

the forerunner of the bank branch of the future, perhaps replacing up to 75 per cent of the sometimes friendly human tellers.'[9]

That's not how things played out.

Bank teller jobs didn't just survive, they roughly doubled between 1970 and 2010, while ATM technology became ubiquitous.[10] What the early predictions got wrong is that they confused tasks with jobs.

Before ATMs, tellers spent much of their days on Bucket 1 tasks: counting bills, processing deposits, handling routine transactions. When machines took over these tasks, something unexpected happened. The jobs didn't go away. They changed, with the remaining tasks, including a lot of Bucket 3 tasks, becoming more valuable.

As economist James Bessen observed, at the same time that ATMs were on the rise, banks were pushing to increase market share through 'relationship banking.'[11] Tellers who once counted cash suddenly had new time to notice when the nervous retiree needed help understanding reverse mortgages, to sense when the frustrated entrepreneur was ready for a business line of credit, or to connect human needs with financial solutions.

These Bucket 3 capabilities that bank tellers had been using to read between the lines, build trust, and solve complex problems became the job's core value. The tellers who recognized this shift and leaned into their human advantages found new opportunities in the midst of disruption.

David Autor, an economist from MIT, made this point well in a recent TED Talk: 'Automating some subset of a position's tasks doesn't make the other ones unnecessary — in fact, it makes them more important and increases their economic value.'[12]

Ultimately, after decades of growth despite ATMs, bank teller jobs finally did start declining in the 2010s.[13] But it wasn't the cash machines that disrupted them. It was the smartphone in your pocket.

When experts in the 1970s were predicting ATMs would all but end bank teller jobs, they couldn't imagine that those jobs would one day be disrupted by millions of people carrying supercomputers in their pockets. Because of the smartphone, so many of us now check balances over a meal, deposit checks with a photo, and transfer money with a tap.

There's a lot for us to learn from bank tellers about managing change. We humans often have a hard time predicting exactly how new technologies will reshape our work, which is why adapting beats predicting right now. You can't reliably forecast which innovation will upend your industry or company or job, but you can build the human capabilities that will matter regardless.

The bank tellers who succeeded across these waves of change were the ones who leaned into what made them irreplaceably human. They reimagined their role based on tasks, not title.

Now it's our turn to reimagine not just our jobs but our careers. And that career ladder you've been climbing? It's getting upended, rung by rung. The playbook your mentors handed down, the one that says to put in your time, follow the path, and wait your turn? That playbook assumes a stability that no longer exists.

Jobs Are Tasks, Not Titles

Hearing that may seem overwhelming, but it can also be freeing. Maybe you can stop trying to climb as fast as possible up a ladder that's falling apart and instead start to let go entirely. If you do, you'll want to grab onto something that rewards creativity over conformity and turns your unique combination of experiences into your greatest strength.

That's where we're going next, as we look at how careers themselves are being reinvented.

The Bottom Line

1. **Your job is not your title.** Letting go of our focus on titles, even just in our own minds, offers freedom to see our jobs for what they are and to leverage our skills accordingly. You're not just a financial analyst, a plumber, or a nurse practitioner. You're a collection of distinctly human capabilities, contributions, and potential that no title could ever capture.

2. **AI is coming for tasks, not jobs.** The three-bucket framework reveals where you stand in your job today: Bucket 1 tasks (what AI can do alone) can be moved off your plate, Bucket 2 tasks (human plus AI) are your immediate opportunity, and Bucket 3 tasks (uniquely human) are your more durable advantage. Success means actively moving work from Bucket 1 to 2, and building up your tasks in Bucket 3.

OPEN TO WORK

3. **Adaptability is key.** Like bank tellers who shifted from dispensing cash to solving customer problems, your ability to adapt is key. And adapting will serve you better than predicting.

CHAPTER 6

Careers Are Climbing Walls, Not Ladders

Maureen Beck, who goes by Mo, was born without her left hand.[1] As she told an audience at the Rox Climbing Festival in 2023, 'I came out screaming and lopsided.'[2]

From day one, Mo's parents refused to treat her differently. They insisted she learn to tie her shoes before kindergarten so no one would tease her. The message was clear: You may have to work differently and harder, but you are capable.

Mo was twelve years old and at summer camp when a counselor suggested she skip the rock-climbing activity. 'Oh, you only have one hand,' she recalls the counselor saying. 'You can sit this one out.' Mo was used to hearing this kind of dismissal and dismissing it right back. She'd thrown and caught baseballs bare-handed after a gym teacher said she couldn't play without a mitt, leaving her with 'a bruised and stinging palm for two weeks.'[3]

So she climbed anyway. And found her calling.

'This rock didn't care that I was a twelve-year-old girl. It didn't care that I had a disability,' Mo told that same audience.

OPEN TO WORK

'I had to invent my way of climbing because, not to date myself, this was before we could just google how to do something.'

Today, Mo is a ten-time national climbing champion, tackling routes most climbers with two hands can't finish, sometimes jamming her shortened left arm into a crack while her right hand searches for the next hold. Twelve-year-old Mo was absolutely right: The rock face doesn't care about her difference.[4]

Where others follow established sequences, she invents new ones. She climbs down to find better angles. Traverses sideways where others power straight up. Uses her feet like extra hands, her shoulder as a pivot point, her entire body as a tool.

Mo has come to realize that the path up a climbing wall is a puzzle with multiple solutions. The best way for you to climb it will be unique to *you*.

This is exactly where you are with your career right now. In the last chapter, you sorted the tasks of your job into buckets, identified your vulnerabilities, and found where your opportunities lie. That's a vital short-term move. Looking further out, we're confronting another reality, this time about careers. When work itself is being reshaped by forces like AI, the career ladder you expected to climb, with its predictable rungs and clear direction, is going to be upended.

What will take its place?

We think what you will climb will look less like a ladder and more like a climbing wall, rewarding everything Mo brings to her climbs: resilience, creative problem-solving, the ability to move in any direction, the courage to forge your own path when the standard ones don't fit.

Think about what Mo's story reveals about a climbing wall. Unlike ladders with their fixed rungs, a climbing wall offers many ways up. Where you place your hand, which direction you move, even whether you go up, down, or sideways, all depends on your unique goals and strengths and what the moment demands. Mo doesn't climb like anyone else because she can't. That constraint became her advantage, allowing her to see possibilities others miss.

That's exactly what's coming for careers. The predictable, even predetermined paths are getting upended. Instead, we're looking at a world of work that will start rewarding the same things that make Mo a champion: finding your own way, using what makes you different, and defining success on your terms.

The Ladder Was Never Meant to Last

For most of human history, careers actually looked nothing like ladders. Before the industrial age, for those who were able to do work that allowed for what we'd consider to be careers, it was all quite entrepreneurial. Craftspeople owned their own tools and merchants managed their own shops.

Even those in what were considered 'professions' had to be entrepreneurial. Doctors made house calls, lawyers took cases as they came, teachers tutored in homes. Success meant building a reputation in your community, adapting to seasonal rhythms, and solving whatever problems arose. Work, for these individuals, was personal, flexible, and largely self-directed.

That all changed with the dawn of the industrial age. Factories didn't need self-directed professionals. They needed workers who showed up at set times and stayed at their stations: interchangeable people doing predictable tasks. And so created the environment that helped the career ladder emerge.

The years following World War II solidified this idea. People joined a large corporation after college, offering loyalty in exchange for job security, climbed steadily for decades, and then eventually retired with a pension and a gold watch. William H. Whyte captured this world in his 1956 book *The Organization Man*.[5] General Motors, known as a 'womb to tomb' employer, epitomized it.

Things began to change over the last generation or so. 'Downsizing' entered the vocabulary in the 1980s, and loyalty to an employer stopped guaranteeing security. Then the internet arrived and upended even the most basic assumptions of career mobility. Why climb a ladder for twenty years when a startup could change your life in two? LinkedIn's own research shows a new pattern playing out: Professionals joining the workforce in 2025 are on pace to hold twice the number of jobs over the course of their careers as the generation that started before them fifteen years ago.[6]

Forward-thinking researchers saw this coming.

Back in 1976, the psychologist Douglas Hall predicted that the future of work would be driven by people having 'protean careers,' paths shaped by you as an individual, your values,

Careers Are Climbing Walls, Not Ladders

your curiosity, and your adaptability.[7] Named after Proteus, the Greek sea-god who could change his form at will, these careers would be self-directed and purpose-driven.

In the early 1900s, a new line of thinking on work started to emerge. Management thinker Charles Handy's observation that more workers were building careers based on multiple income streams and identities.[8] These individuals didn't have one job for one company, but rather a collection of projects, roles, and ventures that evolved over time. He called these 'portfolio careers.' Alongside that term, professors Michael B. Arthur and Denise Rousseau coined the phrase 'boundaryless careers' to describe the way a person's working life was less and less defined by allegiance to a single company and more by flexibility and unpredictability.[9]

Getting a bit more into the details of this phenomenon, the London Business School professor Herminia Ibarra's work in the early 2000s on 'working identity' showed that successful career transitions happen through exploration and experimentation.[10] Her studies of hundreds of career changers found that the best pivots came from trying on new professional identities, not from careful planning alone.

More recently, career development experts Helen Tupper and Sarah Ellis coined the term 'squiggly careers' to describe paths that twist and turn rather than go straight up.[11] Their careers at Microsoft, Virgin, and other companies helped them come to the realization that the most fulfilled workers were creating their own route through continuous experimentation and learning rather than following predetermined paths.

What all these frameworks share is a recognition that careers shouldn't be seen as linear anymore. They're self-driven, creative explorations. Today, the question isn't whether you'll have a nonlinear career. It's whether you'll navigate it by accident or by design.

The Climbing Wall

Ethan Evans is one of LinkedIn's Top Voices on career development, offering courses and advice on how to navigate work in an age of constant change. He also coaches individuals one-on-one and publishes a popular newsletter, all focused on helping people build careers that work for them, not for some outdated playbook.

Ethan's understanding of careers doesn't just come from coaching others or building a nonlinear career himself. It also comes from being a rock climber, which means he knows firsthand why the climbing wall metaphor resonates: Every climb is different, every climber brings something unique, and the route that works for one person won't work for another.

His own career followed that pattern, though he didn't see it that way at first.

Ethan was trained as an engineer, but quickly realized that traditional engineering was not for him. 'I personally found that while I like technology puzzles, the human puzzle of trying to select, bring together, and motivate a team to deliver something was more interesting and compelling to me. So I pivoted very early in my career to a management track, but with no education in that. I had to teach myself.'[12]

That was Ethan's first career pivot. Not up or down, but sideways. From engineer to manager. Looking back, he can see that moment clearly now: He was discovering what energized him as opposed to what drained him.

Ethan spent the next decade working in various operations and management roles at three different startups before landing at Amazon, where he spent fifteen years. As he got further into his career, he found himself 'investing more and more into developing [his] team; being a mentor while being a leader.'

Back when Ethan was studying engineering, he thought he'd become a college professor. 'I've always sort of had the teaching mindset,' he says. 'But I didn't have a PhD in my heart. I got into graduate school, and I saw one of my office mates who had been working on his PhD for eight years and I thought, You know what? I don't have eight years of school left in me.'

Ethan chose industry over academia, but his passion for teaching came with him. As he reflected on his career in the corporate world, he saw that his skill as a teacher was something he wanted to explore further.

'In my job at Amazon, I first started mentoring more people, but then there's a limit to how many people you can mentor at once, because it's very one-on-one,' Ethan says. 'I had a very demanding Amazon job with hundreds of employees, so how much time could I carve off? So that led me to start doing more through writing and public speaking because those are one-to-many.'

OPEN TO WORK

Eventually, Ethan felt his work at Amazon was no longer challenging him in the ways he wanted to be challenged. 'It was possible to move up again at Amazon,' he says, 'but it looked very hard. And it was now less interesting to me because I was making the money I wanted and so on. So that led me to think, I've been climbing this career ladder all my life. If I'm not going to do that, what am I going to do?'

The *why* of Ethan's career, the motivation behind it, was changing. He had financial security; now he wanted something else. He had to figure out precisely what that was. Ethan leaned into what he loved most about his job: coaching. He brought together his former ambitions as an academic, his years of experience as a manager, and his particular skill as a mentor, which he had honed over decades. In 2020, he left Amazon and became a full-time career coach.

What Ethan discovered is that successful climbing isn't about following someone else's path.

'If you're going to succeed at your own climbing wall,' Ethan says, 'you need to start thinking about your gifts and where people might pay for them.' He gives himself as an example: 'I realized that I had gifts for teaching, public speaking, and coaching leaders. I loved to do these things, so they energized me rather than drained me. Once I realized this, I started thinking about how to make them my future business.'

That's exactly the framework we want to give you: the three questions you'll have to think through again and again as you go build and strengthen your career in this new world of work.

The Three Questions

Let's start by saying that you will have to put in some new work with this new mindset. If you're designing your career yourself, you have to define it for yourself too. You have to develop it based on who you are and what you want. We can't do that for you, and you wouldn't want us to, but we can break it down into manageable pieces, Gene Kranz style. To shape your career as you live it, you need to be thinking about *why* you work, *what* you uniquely do, and *where* you want to go.

You won't just do this once and be done with it. As work keeps changing, as technology keeps changing, as your own thoughts about your career and your life keep changing, your answers to these questions will change too. Sometimes you may know the answer to one and not the other. Sometimes you may be focusing on one at the expense of the other. That's all okay. You're figuring it out as you go. You're adapting. You're adjusting. What's important is that along the way, you'll start creating a career that is unique to you, one that's never been done before because it's one that only you can do.

OPEN TO WORK

Question 1: *Why* Do You Work?

In the ladder world, success was often defined and controlled by others: the next rung, then the next rung, then maybe the manager role, then maybe the team lead role, then maybe, eventually, a corner office, all tied to salary benchmarks and promotions that you either got or didn't. On the climbing wall, you define success on your terms. So this first question is about defining what success is for you, based not on the expectations of your family, your industry, or society in general, but on what you want for yourself.

For many people, the *why* is pretty straightforward. And understandably so. The goal at work is to earn enough money to support yourself and your family: to give your kids opportunities you didn't have or to afford to do the things in life you most want to do. Financial security, especially if you've grown up without it, is often the most powerful *why* around. But beyond that, maybe what motivates you is building something new or helping a sector advance or a community grow. Maybe it's mastering a craft or leading a team.

Whatever your *why*, there's no wrong answer, but there is a wrong approach: climbing for someone else's reasons. 'People who know their *why* climb better,' says Ethan.

As the ladder falls, your success is going to stem more and more from solving problems only you can solve. This makes defining your *why* more important than ever, because your intrinsic motivation will need to become one of your biggest advantages. That internal drive, the curiosity that keeps you learning, the hunger that makes you push through setbacks, the genuine care that helps you see what others miss, is an important competitive edge. And it can be an anchor that keeps you steady when the world around you shifts because of technological change.

Figuring out your *why* isn't a onetime exercise. As things change and you change, your definition of success is likely to evolve. Having clarity about *why* you want your career to look a certain way, even as that *why* deepens or shifts, gives you the foundation to make every other decision with purpose. It's the benchmark you can hold every decision to. Does this contribute to my *why* or detract from it? Has my *why* changed?

Jonetta, the fifty-six-year-old AI-skeptic-turned-advocate, knew she was climbing not to 'work a job,' as she felt her mother had done, but to have a career.[13] Being a nurse felt like a career to her. Decades later, so did being a project manager. She wanted to be able to grow within her roles: to feel she was constantly learning and being challenged. As she grew older, a better schedule, better benefits, and a better salary began to matter more to her too. She notes that as she gets 'more and more golden,' she doesn't 'want to be pinching pennies.'

'It is rare that what motivates someone at twenty will remain constant until fifty or sixty,' says Ethan. 'The *why* changes. Perhaps, initially, I climb towards financial security, or work-life balance. Then maybe I pivot to a *why* of personal meaning.'

Question 2: *What* Do You Uniquely Do?

Now that you understand your *why*, you need to identify your *what*. By that we mean the unique combination of capabilities, skills, and experiences you bring to your work. This builds directly on chapter 5's three buckets. You've already sorted what AI can do, what you'll do with AI, and what only you can do. Now ask yourself: What do those buckets reveal about you?

Look for patterns. Which capabilities show up repeatedly in your Bucket 2 and Bucket 3 work? Which tasks energize you? Which drain you? What problems do people consistently ask you to solve? Those things are *what* you uniquely do, most often not just with individual skills but with a mix of skills.

'List your best skills, then look where several overlap,' says Ethan. 'While you may not be the best at any one skill, you may be among the very best at the combination. That's the *what* that no one else can match.'

Take Ume, the computer programmer and coding influencer. She discovered she didn't have to choose between technical ability and communication skills, treating one as real and the other as secondary. Her unique combination of technical expertise, teaching ability, and her perspective as a young woman in tech creates value few others can offer. The ladder would have forced her to pick a lane. The wall lets her use everything she brings.

When you find work that aligns with your unique mix, everything changes. As Ethan puts it: 'If you're doing work you love, work you'd happily do for free, then it's not work but play. Someone who views the same tasks as work can never compete with someone who loves it, because work wears us out and play doesn't.'

Your *what* will evolve as AI reshapes the *what* of work for us all. So keep revisiting your buckets. The more deliberately you map your tasks to underlying capabilities, the steadier you'll be when things shift.

And when AI makes a strength less relevant?

'Ask what AI lets you do better that can become part of a new *what*,' Ethan suggests. 'Probably there is something you have wanted to do but haven't because a weakness in one area has held you back. The great thing about intersecting skills is that you do not need to be the very best at any of them; you only need to be the best in your unique combination. If AI can help you move from poor to good in an area, that may be enough to unlock all kinds of new combinations with your other skills.'

Just as claiming your *why* isn't a onetime exercise, finding your *what* isn't, either. The technical skills that once set you apart early in your career may become table stakes as you advance. What distinguishes you as a junior analyst will be entirely different from what distinguishes you as a senior leader. Each new challenge, new role, or new project you take on should expand your *what*.

OPEN TO WORK

Question 3: *Where* Do You Want to Go?

The ladder had basically one destination: directly up from one rung to the next. The new world of work will likely offer many more paths that can lead in many more directions. The goal is to find *where* your unique capabilities meet real problems that matter to you and that the world wants to solve.

Where starts, in a literal sense, with where you work. Especially if you're early in your career, the place you work right now matters a lot. You want to be in organizations that are embracing this moment of change rather than resisting it. You want to be at a company that invests in your growth, allows you to experiment with AI, and helps you develop an understanding of how your job and career are going to evolve.

Ultimately, though, where you work today should serve *where* you're trying to go in your career. That's the key to this question.

Take Taj English from chapter 2, the founder of ListedB. The *why* of his climb, what inspired him every day, was finding a way to build financial security while also impacting his community. *What* he could uniquely do was a mix of things. He knew how to work with technology. He knew how to build things from scratch. And he knew his community. From there, his *where* became clear: building technology and a company that serves his community.

Whenever you're feeling stuck or overwhelmed, AI can help you discover possible *wheres* by pointing out jobs and opportunities you might not have thought of or found on your own.

Again, AI is both a force for change and a tool for change. At LinkedIn, we've built a job search feature powered by AI where you can express what you want in a job in your own words. For example, 'I want to use my marketing skills to cure cancer' or 'I'm looking for business development roles that let me work on video games.'

Instead of puzzling over the perfect wording for a job title or the perfect keywords for a job type in your search, AI can interpret the meaning behind your words and deliver relevant matches for you, including ones you might have overlooked before.

Deciding *where* you are going is iterative. You'll adjust, pivot, and sometimes completely reimagine your destination as work shifts. Consider Ethan, who spent more than a decade climbing traditional corporate ladders at Amazon. He achieved financial security, which was one version of his *why*, but then, as his *why* evolved to 'pay forward my good fortune by helping others find both career success and satisfaction,' he created a new *where*: building a successful coaching business.

The Two Forces

So, those are the key questions to always have in mind: *why* you work, *what* you uniquely do, and *where* you want to go. Each of those questions should be an ongoing conversation with yourself as work changes and your life unfolds. Your *why* might shift from seeking growth to seeking security. Your *what* might expand as AI unlocks new capabilities. Your *where* might change as you arrive at one destination and set your sights on another.

That's a lot in itself, but alongside all that, you will also want to keep in mind two big forces that will shape all of our careers from here on out.

Force 1: Think Like an Entrepreneur

Paul Cheek, the entrepreneurship expert at MIT, said it best: For most of us, 'entrepreneur' feels like a title for other people. It describes the risk-takers who have resources we don't, or the tech wizards who can code all night. Many of us think that being an entrepreneur is for naturals who somehow know how to raise money, hire teams, and scale businesses. It requires things most of us don't have, like capital, connections, or even just the stomach for that kind of uncertainty.

In this new era for our economy, entrepreneurialism isn't just for founders in Silicon Valley. It's going to be a way of work that we all will have to tap into: a habit of testing ideas, adjusting quickly, and turning constraints into opportunities.

In many ways, entrepreneurialism is tied to the adaptability we mentioned in the previous chapter. And to the 5Cs we discussed in chapter 3. Having the curiosity to spot opportunities others miss. The courage to build something that doesn't exist. The creativity to see constraints as challenges, not roadblocks. The compassion to solve real problems for real people. The communication skills to bring others along on the journey.

Remember the definition of entrepreneurial that Paul proposes. Being entrepreneurial is just about creating more than is reasonable with the resources that we have control of. To be more entrepreneurial at work, you don't need anything more than what you have. You just need to start to think like an entrepreneur while looking at what you have.

'Teaching entrepreneurship is teaching agency,' Paul says. 'Giving people agency, the mindset, and the skill set to turn something that is wildly uncertain into something that is concrete. Taking an idea and turning it into impact.'[14]

'If we can empower people to do that,' Paul says, 'whether in the context of a startup or in the context of their personal life or a corporate role, we all of a sudden empower them to move the needle either for the organization that they're a part of [in] their personal life or for impact in society. If we can teach them to move the needle, they are going to have an impact in society. That's what I want to empower people to do, regardless of whether they choose to start a new company or not. And using AI allows them to accelerate that process in ways that were obviously not possible before.'

Diego A. Rubio discovered the opportunities of entrepreneurialism when traditional paths failed him. Growing up in rural Texas, he watched his father lose his transportation business in 2008 and move three hours away to the oil fields, which was the only work available to him. When Diego later dropped out of college and couldn't get hired due to degree requirements, he chose what he calls the 'permissionless' path.[15]

'Entrepreneurship is the only avenue that doesn't ask for permission,' he says.

OPEN TO WORK

In 2017, Diego started a recruiting company. No permission needed. No credentials required. Just the grit to figure it out as he went. 'Once you label yourself a business owner, an entrepreneur, nobody questions it,' he explains. 'As long as you're doing it and proving it, there's no piece of paper that says you're an expert.'

Since then, Diego has been helping others access opportunity through entrepreneurship. In particular, he helps other rural entrepreneurs use AI to build businesses, so that other families don't have to live apart for the sake of a paycheck.

'Now you don't need a software developer; you just need a prompt to build the app that you want,' Diego says. When rural entrepreneurs can access the same tools as their urban counterparts, they don't have to choose between opportunity and home. They can build businesses where they are, creating the economic foundation that keeps communities intact.

Diego's not alone: The number of LinkedIn members adding 'founder' and related titles to their profiles jumped up 67 percent from 2024 to 2025 across ten major economies.[16] Meanwhile, there's been a similar uptick in conversations on the LinkedIn feed about entrepreneurship, particularly in India, Sweden, and the UAE, as more people start to explore what striking out on their own might look like.

As Paul points out, you no longer need to raise capital in order to think like an entrepreneur. You just need to approach your career as a builder: Start where you are, use what you have, test ideas quickly, learn from what doesn't work, and keep moving.

This will be increasingly important as hiring and promotion become less based on where you went to school, what degree you have, or what jobs you've done in the past, and more on what you have built for yourself and others, at your workplace or in your garage.

In this new era, your work product is the new résumé. The actual projects, results, and contributions you have made are what employers will look for to see what you can do. How entrepreneurial you are and what you have created are all going to be core to your value-add.

At LinkedIn, we're testing this out ourselves with initiatives like our Associate Product Builder program, where we're hiring entry-level talent to learn every step of the process of building. We've redesigned the hiring process for this program. The first thing prospective builders submit isn't their résumés; it's something they've built so we can see what they can do, not simply where they have been.

Force 2: Your Network Is Your Navigation System

We've all heard some version of this piece of advice: 'It's not what you know; it's who you know.' Raj Chetty's research at Harvard confirms this. Your network supports and inspires you, and helps you understand what is possible for your career.

On the ladder, networks were mostly vertical. You looked up for sponsors and mentors, for people who could help you rise to the next rung. On the wall, your network becomes multidirectional. You still need mentors who've already climbed similar routes and can share hard-won wisdom about terrain you haven't encountered yet. You still need sponsors who go beyond advice to actions, people with the power to hire, promote, or fund your next move, opening doors and advocating for you in rooms where you're not present. But you also need peers and pacing partners.

In this new world, some of your most valuable connections might now be people pursuing similar paths, giving you real-time signals about opportunities and obstacles from their vantage point. These fellow climbers aren't just sources of information; they're potential collaborators and partners. You're meeting people whose moves complement yours, whose strengths balance your gaps, whose vision aligns with where you want to go. You might find yourself working with them, for them, or hiring them. Or they might become your referral network if you start your own business. As Ethan says, 'The network is like a spotter, who can tell us what lies out of our immediate sight: the clients, partners, new roles, and opportunities that can make our next move. In climbing, this is called "beta" information from others about the paths up the wall and the tricky moves and ways to work around them.'

Here are some things to think about as you focus on networks:

If you aren't starting with a strong network, you can start to build one anytime. Just be thoughtful. Don't lead with what you need; lead with what you can offer. Can you research something for someone? Help organize an event? Share insights from your unique perspective? Value flows both ways in healthy networks.

Careers Are Climbing Walls, Not Ladders

Join communities built around learning. Professional associations, LinkedIn groups, and skill-building programs help level the playing field because everyone's there to grow together. Merit America, where Jonetta found her tech training, isn't just about skills; it's about connecting people to networks they wouldn't otherwise be able to access.

Think deliberately about more casual connections, like that colleague from three jobs ago, or the person you met at a conference. Those weaker ties often provide the most surprising opportunities because they move in different circles from your close contacts.

Help yourself be found by others by writing, speaking, teaching, or building something that demonstrates your expertise. When you create value publicly, networks start forming around you without you needing to chase them.

'This is exactly how I built my network,' Ethan says. 'I started sharing what I knew, posting on LinkedIn. I went from the normal network most people have, of former classmates and coworkers, maybe a thousand people, to over one hundred fifty thousand people who valued that advice. Now, I have that huge army of people I can call on when I need something. I have connections in almost every field and every country on earth.'

When it comes to networking in this new age, think of it this way: Being entrepreneurial makes you look inward and find your unique edge. Your network makes you look outward and rewards you for bringing the real version of yourself to your career. For the first time, these two forces are pushing in the same direction, creating real opportunity for people who lean into it.

OPEN TO WORK

At this point in the book, we want to acknowledge something really important. Engaging in this moment of big change is necessary. Without that, we cannot shape how this change plays out for us or our communities. But being engaged as an individual is not enough.

You can master the three-bucket framework. You can develop durable skills. You can even start shifting how you think about your career. You can do all of that, but if your company or industry, or even the economy itself, isn't also adapting, there's only so much you can do on your own.

That's where we turn to next as we go from the individual to the institution. Your success in this new era isn't just about how well you climb. It's also about how well the structures around you shift to support the new ways of work.

The Bottom Line

1. **Your career is now a climbing wall, not a ladder.**
   The predictable path is gone, replaced by multiple routes that will reward creativity over conformity. Just as Mo Beck invented new climbing techniques, you'll invent new career sequences that turn your unique combination of skills and interests into advantages.

Careers Are Climbing Walls, Not Ladders

2. **Think like an entrepreneur, even if you never start a company.** Seeing constraints as opportunities, building with what you have, and learning from failure aren't optional anymore. Being entrepreneurial is key to succeeding in this new era for work.

3. **Your network is your navigation system.** You are not climbing the wall alone. Many of your peers might be climbing parallel routes, spotting obstacles or opportunities you might have missed. If you aren't starting with a strong network, you can start to build one anytime.

CHAPTER 7

Companies Are Work Charts, Not Org Charts

In the 1890s, factory owners had electricity all wrong.[1] When they first installed electric motors, many treated them like better steam engines.[2] That was certainly true at the Boston Bank Note and Lithograph Company.[3] In 1890, they ripped out their old steam engine and plugged in an electric one, but changed nothing else. The printing presses stayed put. The paper-cutting machines remained in their corners. Even the old belts and pulleys that had connected everything to steam power stayed in place, now just hitched to electricity.

The trade press celebrated this upgrade, praising electricity's 'steady and reliable power.'[4] And, yes, print quality improved. Productivity, on the other hand, barely budged.

Factory owners, having sunk lots of money into the latest big new technology, grumbled that electricity was all hype, no payoff. The economist Paul David later explained why: They were 'doubling-up' by overlaying a new technology onto an old system, like putting a sports car engine into a horse-drawn carriage.

Then a few pioneers asked the question that started to change everything: What if we didn't just electrify the old way of working? What if we rebuilt work itself around the possibilities of electricity?

Their answer seemed radical to many at the time because of what it required: tearing down the multistory factories. Building single-story layouts.[5] Giving every worker their own motor and their own switch. Letting work flow in straight lines instead of snaking around drive shafts.[6] In short, it required a total culture change, not just a floor-plan redesign. New training. New contracts. New ways of thinking about everyone's role on the factory floor.

By the 1920s, these reimagined factories were no longer seen as radical. They were seen as successful. They saw productivity surge past 5 percent annual growth,[7] which was much higher than other industries at the time and a rate unmatched in earlier or later years.

The lesson economist Paul David drew from studying this transformation was that revolutionary technology alone changes little. Real transformation happens when we stop forcing new tools into old patterns and start asking what's possible, now, that was never possible before.[8]

Today, every company faces a choice similar to the one factory owners faced. You can bolt AI onto existing structures and hope for the best, or you can fundamentally rebuild the structures around AI.

To do that will, once again, require a total culture change, not just a floor-plan redesign. That's why, just as we introduced a new way to think about careers in the last chapter, in

Companies Are Work Charts, Not Org Charts

this chapter we are introducing a new way to think about the structure of work itself.

The org chart, which is that familiar pyramid of boxes and reporting lines, was designed for the industrial era. It told everyone where they fit, whom they answered to, and what lane they stayed in. Predictability was the point.

In an AI-powered world, predictability isn't really possible. The work itself will keep shifting. Projects will get stood up and then dissolved. Skills will combine in new ways across the lines that currently separate functions like sales and marketing. The rigid hierarchy that once created order now threatens to become a barrier to the very agility companies need most.

Microsoft calls the alternative a 'work chart,' which means organizing not around fixed positions but around the work that needs doing.[9] Instead of asking 'who reports to whom?' the alternative asks 'who needs to collaborate on what?' Like the shift from central power plants to distributed electricity, it's about letting capability flow where it's needed, when it's needed.

At LinkedIn, we've been intentional in trying to understand this transformation from the inside out at all kinds of companies. Talent leaders, chief human resource officers, and chief people officers are key partners for our business. Over the past few years, we have spent significant time sitting down with them all over the world. Our understanding of the shifts companies need to undertake is informed by these honest and open conversations.

Whether or not companies are able to pull off this transformation from org chart to work chart is likely to determine which companies get ahead in the AI era and which companies fall behind. Perfection isn't the goal. As Eric Dozier, chief people officer at Eli Lilly, told us: 'As long as we can iterate, we don't have to be perfect. Let's embrace and launch things.'[10]

That willingness to iterate reveals something crucial. The real challenge here isn't technical. AI tools are remarkably simple to learn. The real challenge is human. It's about letting go of the hierarchies that are dated even if they feel comfortable. It's about trusting employees to self-organize around problems. It's about accepting that the org chart, which told us exactly where we belonged, must give way to something more dynamic.

Companies don't struggle with AI because the technology is hard. They struggle because changing how humans work together is harder.

A Complete and Total Behavioral Shift

When Conor Grennan[11] first encountered AI in his role as dean of students at NYU's Stern School of Business, he says his immediate thought was, 'This is going to disrupt absolutely everything.' He was right, and it started with his own career.

Initially, Conor built a curriculum to teach his students how to use AI in the context of business. He wanted that curriculum to be as useful as possible to his students, so he went to businesses around New York and asked them how they were using AI. The answer was that they mostly weren't.

So he decided that he would teach businesses how to use AI and return in a few months to find out what they were doing with it. That would give him helpful information that he could bring back to his students and add to his curriculum.

It wasn't that hard to teach leadership teams how to use AI, he says. 'There's nothing to learn. All you have to do is talk,' he adds with a smile. 'My background is not in technology at all. I have no technical background whatsoever.'

It turned out that understanding how businesses use AI, how they misuse it, and what stumbling blocks they encounter along the way has less to do with technology than you would imagine. When Conor returned to all those businesses after some time, they still mostly weren't using AI. And if they were, they were using it in exactly the ways he had taught them: employing it for the handful of examples he had demonstrated in his lesson, and nowhere else.

'I realized that there was something very different and unique about this technology,' says Conor, 'because there didn't seem to be anything to learn whatsoever. And yet people did not seem to be picking it up as I thought they should be. If there's nothing to learn, everybody could just start using it, yet, they weren't. So what was stopping them? And that led us down this giant path where we are now today, which is realizing that this was actually not a learning curve at all. This was a complete and total behavioral shift.'

A complete and total behavioral shift isn't ultimately about technology. It's about psychology. It's about management. It's about corporate culture. Conor knows about those fields. He was dean of students at a business school, after all. Given his role, he wanted to learn more about the phenomenon he saw playing out across offices in New York. That's how Conor found himself as Stern's first ever chief AI architect.

Conor emphasizes that the change that is coming to work is 'not really a digital transformation at all. It's really change management.

'Digital transformation,' he explains, 'is where you take an old technology and replace it with a new technology … You're not replacing anything here … It's not paper and pencil, and now you have Excel. Or, you used to have the fax machine, and now you have email. All those things are linear progressions of the same type of technology, or it's a new technology accomplishing the same thing just more efficiently.'

Conor says that when he goes to companies and asks groups the question of what AI replaces, 'there's simply no good answer for it. You know, there's bad answers: Oh, it replaces junior-level talent, or it replaces your brain, or it replaces Google, but none of these things really answer the question of what it replaces.

'That's because this is not a technology that works in the same way any technology in the past has ever worked,' Conor notes. Historically, he says, technological innovators generally understood what the jobs of the future would be. If you invented the steam engine, you knew you needed someone to shovel coal and someone to maintain the parts. Technology dictated the jobs.

Conor sees AI as breaking the pattern. Company leaders, even at technology companies, don't know what the jobs of the future will look like. 'The only people that are going to figure this out are the people doing the jobs,' says Conor. 'And that's very, very different from anything we've ever seen before.'

In Conor's mind, innovation isn't going to come from the top down. It's going to come from all over an organization. That's why it's critical for leaders to be pro-human in this moment, not just pro-AI. So how do companies organize for that?

From Org Chart to Work Chart

In the mid-1800s, Daniel McCallum faced a problem that arose with the industrial age. He needed to make a sprawling, complex organization more efficient. As general manager of the New York and Erie Railroad, he oversaw hundreds of miles of track, countless workers, and operations that sprawled beyond what any one person could see or control.[12] He had to ensure that work flowed predictably, so that he wouldn't have to oversee every little detail, which was an impossible task.

His solution was perhaps the world's first organizational chart. McCallum didn't draw it the way we do today. Instead of a pyramid with leadership at the top, he created an upward-growing tree, with leadership at the roots and branches spreading above. His chart emphasized support and information flow, not just hierarchy. It also made visible who was responsible for what, putting on paper the intricacies of a system too complex to hold in any one mind.

OPEN TO WORK

For the next century and a half, this innovation became a cornerstone of management. Frederick Taylor and Henri Fayol, the philosophical fathers of modern management, refined the concept into the command-and-control pyramids we know today. The org chart became as fundamental to business as the balance sheet. For generations.

And then came AI.

When companies first encounter AI, they tend to do what they've always done with new technology: They find a box for it on the org chart. 'Let's build an AI Center of Excellence!' the CEO announces. It seems smart. Strategic. Like what you need to do to take this seriously.

This approach reveals why most AI initiatives stall before they start. The org chart wasn't built for dynamism, and in a world where AI democratizes innovation, that's a fatal flaw. Because when anyone can use AI without specialized training, innovation can come from anywhere in the organization, not simply from leadership.

This is where the work chart comes in and why this evolution in how a company is organized matters. Where org charts organize around positions, work charts organize around outcomes. Where org charts create hierarchies, work charts create networks. Where org charts freeze structures in place, work charts allow them to evolve.

Conor backs this up. 'You don't know where in your organization people are going to be amazing at [using AI],' he says. 'Because it's extremely democratized, there's nothing to learn. All you have to do is talk. So you can't even identify them coming in, you can't tell by their résumés, you can't tell by anything other than, Are they using it or not?'

At LinkedIn, we've used similar thinking to change how engineers build by adopting what we call a Full Stack Builder model. What once required coordination across multiple functions, from product managers to UX designers to front-end engineers to back-end engineers to QA specialists, now happens seamlessly as a process between a single builder and their AI tools. As a result, people spend less time managing handoffs from one team to the next, and more time building and launching products from the ground up.

Microsoft's Work Trend Index, their annual report on the trends shaping the world at work, captures the shift well. We're moving toward 'a dynamic, outcome-driven model where teams form around goals, not functions.'[13] But the real transformation goes deeper. As Conor explains: 'You upskill everybody. So now you have a company, and I mean this literally, of innovators. Not just, like, Oh, we hired innovators. No, no. You've given everybody the innovation tool.'

Leaders will soon discover what happens when AI meets human entrepreneurialism at scale. 'You're going to be looking across your company,' Conor predicts, 'and you're going to say, like, Oh, over there in building six there's a team of three people doing the work of fourteen. What are they doing?' And you're going to realize quickly that they are employees who understand their work's nuances better than anyone else and have figured out AI integrations no one anticipated.

OPEN TO WORK

There is a challenge to all this: the change management challenge Conor talked about earlier. Humans resist change. We seek comfort in the ways things are, even if that means we are resisting change that is in our interest. Neuroscientist Vivienne Ming discovered in her research that people actively avoid situations that force them to confront what they don't know. Which is why, as Conor emphasizes, success isn't about the technology.[14] 'You could put a treadmill in every house in America, and you're not going to cure heart disease, right? It's not about the tool; it's about whether or not you're going to change behavior.'

The Three Shifts

The work chart, then, isn't simply a new organizational structure. It's a framework for enabling, as Conor calls it, a complete and total behavioral change.

To make this real, organizations need to consider three shifts in how they operate, each building on the other. First, top executives will need to focus more on fostering innovation than securing stability, which will mean leading by design more than command. Second, leadership teams at all levels will need to find new ways to connect existent skills and capabilities across the organization with new types of work and workflow that are going to emerge with AI. Finally, managers, who are perhaps the most critical part of whether someone feels invested in their job or not, will need to go from managing the tasks of their team to coaching the people on their team. That's going to change almost everything about that role.

Let's look at each shift in detail.

Shift 1: Lead by Design, Not Command

Clay Christensen famously warned in *The Innovator's Dilemma* that even successful companies fail when they can't escape the structures that once made them great.[15] He showed that leading firms armed with talented people and well-worn processes repeatedly lost to scrappier competitors, not because they lacked resources or intelligence, but because their organizational structures were built for yesterday's success.

Today's leadership teams face that same choice: redesign the system or watch it calcify around them.

Microsoft provides a good example of the approach that will be key to building a work chart. Rather than just introducing AI tools, the company has fundamentally reshaped its culture and structure. Microsoft got rid of rigid hierarchies and the 'stack ranking' performance system that had often pitted employees against each other. In their place, the company instated flatter, more agile teams centered on customer success and innovation. Microsoft has also championed a learn-it-all mindset and encouraged cross-team collaboration that had been nearly impossible under the old structure.

By removing these barriers, Satya Nadella, Microsoft's CEO since 2014, made it possible for employees to contribute where they could create the most value rather than where the org chart dictated.[16] The results speak to the power of thinking as a designer of more dynamic systems rather than as someone whose job is to maintain a strict organizational structure: Microsoft's market capitalization grew more than tenfold during his first decade as CEO, with rapid advances in AI and cloud services driving this performance.

The push to think differently extends beyond tech companies. Walmart, the nation's largest private employer with more than two million workers globally, faces perhaps one of the most complex organizational redesigns of the AI era. Unlike companies where most employees sit at desks, Walmart's workforce spans stores, warehouses, supply chains, and distribution centers, with many workers in roles that have traditionally seemed protected from technological disruption.

Walmart's approach to the age of AI centers on a big premise: The company sees its distributed workforce as its greatest asset, especially if innovation gets unlocked at every level.[17] Rather than pushing AI tools down from headquarters, the company is fostering collaboration across store managers, associates, and supply chain teams, allowing those closest to customers and daily operations to identify opportunities and experiment with solutions. Store teams are encouraged to run pilots, adapt workflows, and share best practices across regions. Walmart's design creates an organization where innovation can bubble up from the ground.

In the financial sector, Citigroup is designing one of the industry's most comprehensive AI-driven transformations. As

Companies Are Work Charts, Not Org Charts

Citigroup noted in 2025, the company is 'committed to embedding AI into how we work,' a vision that requires rethinking not just technology, but how information flows across the approximately 230,000-person global organization.[18]

Citigroup's leadership team started with the foundation. The bank ditched more than one thousand old software systems, which is the kind of legacy tech that just gets in the way. With that clutter gone, AI could actually do its job. Citi then rolled out AI tools to nearly all employees to help them work smarter, and gave the bank's developers new AI coding tools so they could build better. Already, the tools are freeing up tens of thousands of hours for Citi's developers a week, allowing them to focus on more human work rather than the technical work of writing and reviewing code.

What these leadership teams share is a fundamental shift in how they see their role. They're not managing departments or directing their teams; they're actively and intentionally designing the conditions where innovation can happen and scale quickly. To do that well, they're getting direct feedback from all levels and functions, listening to what everyday employees say they need in order to do their best work, and using that as a compass to build new ways of working.

It's worth noting that this kind of thinking requires prioritizing speed over stability, which is a key difference between the work chart and the org chart. Growth is going to come from how fast companies can adapt, requiring teams to operate more like startups: higher trust, lower egos, fewer approvals, quick stand-ups instead of meetings about meetings. Of course, innovation needs guardrails to stay constructive rather than chaotic, but those guardrails should support the flow of ideas, not block them. Finding that balance is going to be a key part of designing the work charts of the future.

Shift 2: See Capabilities, Not Categories

At most companies, employees are still defined most by the titles they have and the departments they sit in. But that view doesn't come close to capturing the full capabilities of any individual employee. As a result, when you need someone with a specific skill, it can take months to find them and move them, if it ever happens at all.

The examples are everywhere, hiding in plain sight. Could a marketer in the United States apply her fluency in Turkish to help gauge your potential in a new market? Could an analyst with a side gig mixing beats help with music for your new ad campaign? Every company has 'Lost Einsteins' already on payroll, people whose hidden skills never surface because we only see them through the narrow lens of their job titles.

This disconnect between what people can do and what they're assigned to do is one of the great inefficiencies of the labor market. Companies lose talent because great people can't find interesting projects that match their skills. Meanwhile, interesting projects fail because the right people aren't deployed to work on them.

Fixing this is genuinely hard to do. Filtering by degree or job title takes seconds, and has become second nature for many HR teams. Actually understanding someone's capabilities, knowing their real skills and not just their credentials, takes time, expertise, and tools most companies don't have. It's why a 2024 study from Harvard Business School found less than one in seven hundred people in the United States were hired without a degree for jobs that previously required one, despite widespread focus on skills-based hiring.[19]

This is where AI could be transformative. The same technology that's reshaping work could also reshape how we identify talent. AI can analyze work samples, assess problem-solving approaches, and identify patterns in skills demonstrations that humans might miss. It can scale what was previously too labor-intensive: evaluating people based on what they can actually do.

Of course, AI is only as good as how we design and oversee it. Without careful human oversight, these systems risk amplifying existing biases or creating new blind spots. But with that careful oversight, AI can also finally help us address the very real human bias that has embedded itself across the labor market with a preference for the right degree or job title or connection.

Get this right, and we can create something remarkable: a labor market where what you can do matters most when you're up for a job.

The economist and CEO/co-founder of Opportunity@ Work, Byron Auguste, knows what that world looks like, because his father lived it.

Byron's father completed a year of college but had to drop out because he couldn't afford not to work. Working as a shipping clerk, he saw a newspaper ad: 'Learn COBOL and punch your own ticket,' which was a catchy slogan about the IBM computing language transforming business. COBOL was so new there weren't even degrees for it yet. He had never worked in technology, had never even worked in an office, but he decided to check it out.[20]

For six months, Byron's dad studied COBOL while Byron's mother worked to support the family. Byron still keeps a copy of the certificate his father earned from completing that course.

When Byron's mother, who worked at Detroit Edison, arranged for someone in the IT department there to give her husband a chance to shadow them on the job, something remarkable happened. '[My dad] seemed to know some COBOL,' Byron recalled in an interview a few years ago. 'So they hired him into an entry-level programming job. And really, that change was our family's trajectory shift into the American middle class.'[21]

His father became an excellent COBOL programmer, building a career that would have been impossible if employers had required a four-year degree for a skill that universities didn't even teach yet. 'My dad literally could write his own ticket,' Byron says. 'You could get a job anywhere as a COBOL programmer at that time.'

Byron has spent decades studying how the very system that once gave his father a chance has turned into something that would likely exclude him today. His research reveals that by treating bachelor's degrees as prerequisites for skilled employment, employers screen out more than seventy million American workers who are STARs, or people Skilled Through

Alternative Routes. It's a term Byron has worked tirelessly to popularize.

'Smart companies are hiring for potential, not pedigree,' Byron argues. 'If you try to hire the most poachable person, don't be surprised when they are poached.'[22]

Byron sees AI as a mirror that reflects our intentions back at us, amplified. 'Don't blame the tools; fix the rules,' he says. 'If you're trying to screen people out who don't have the pedigree, AI will help you do that. Or, if you're trying to screen people in – who've gained needed skills by a huge variety of routes – AI can help you do that even more. If you allow people to rise based on skills, you will have stronger performance.'

It's important to note here that anything related to skills will need to go beyond technical skills to include the unique human skills that are going to become more valuable, and in some ways essential, in this new era for work. Companies will need to know who demonstrates exceptional empathy in client interactions, who naturally facilitates difficult conversations, who comes up with big ideas under pressure.

This is, of course, harder than it sounds. As we've discussed, over the past century, we've built sophisticated systems for assessing technical skills, whether with certifications, degrees, or proficiency tests. We know how to measure coding ability or accounting expertise. But mapping human capabilities like empathy, creativity, or collaboration? That's newer, mushier territory.

Some pioneers are already starting to crack this code. When researcher Vivienne Ming set out to discover what made computer programmers successful, she stumbled on resilience as the key differentiator. Her work proved that these 'unmeasurable' human qualities could be identified and measured, and that they could matter more than traditional credentials. Now, as AI handles routine work, companies that figure out how to identify, develop, and deploy these human skills will have an enormous advantage.

The foundation of the work chart lies in recognizing people's capabilities rather than prioritizing their fixed job categories. That's what creates the organizational agility necessary for the AI era. No company has this fully figured out yet. The most promising programs are mainly pilots or small-scale experiments. But every transformation starts somewhere, and a great place to begin is actually pretty simple: Start talking about skills.

Ask your teams what they can do beyond their job descriptions. Create forums where people can share hidden capabilities. Make skills growth part of regular one-on-ones. These conversations cost nothing but can reveal everything, whether it's the marketer who speaks Turkish, the analyst who produces music, the 'Lost Einsteins' already on your payroll.

IBM shows where this thinking leads when taken seriously. Under CHRO Nickle LaMoreaux, IBM built its entire review system around three pillars: business results, skills, and behaviors. Skills growth, a measure of what you've learned and its relevance to the business, is now central to every performance discussion. '[We want] employees to understand not just the skills that are needed today, but those that are critical as they go forward,' Nickle explains.[23]

Shift 3: Develop People, Not Tasks

John Wooden won ten NCAA basketball championships in twelve years at UCLA, which is a record that still stands in college basketball.[24] His legacy, however, wasn't simply the trophies. It was also how he changed the way we think about developing human potential. Wooden believed that his job was to produce winning people, not simply winning players. The championships were a byproduct of that focus.

As he said, 'A coach is someone who can give correction without causing resentment.'[25] That's the difference organizations need now. Managers tell people what to do and check whether they did it. Coaches help people figure out what they're capable of and support them as they grow.

This shift has never been more urgent. AI is taking over routine tasks while creating new demands for work centered around creativity and problem-solving. Employees are learning new skills on the fly, watching their jobs transform in real time. LinkedIn's research shows over half the workforce say mastering AI feels like a second job.[26] You can't supervise someone through that transformation. You have to coach them through it.

That makes the role of manager critical right now. Managers at all levels will need to bring people along, address fears, and help individuals see opportunity where they might see only threat. The old way of managing was about delineating tasks, making sure those tasks get done, and ensuring their execution meets a certain standard. The new way of managing is going to be more about developing people, coaching them, and finding new ways to help make sure they are adaptable and up to the challenge that AI poses.

'I find that with AI, coaching is much more important,' says Conor, 'because people have to actually find their own train of thought, and they have to actually find their own drive on this … It's a very hard thing to mandate.'

Remember Conor's earlier insight: The people doing the work know the work best. Managers are going to be critical in motivating teams to innovate and giving them permission to experiment. That's how you get three people in building six doing the work of fourteen.

At LinkedIn, we recently made every employee eligible for professional coaching. As our chief people officer, Teuila Hanson, said, 'We're providing coaching to all employees because we know everyone can benefit from a safe place to receive hands-on, personalized guidance on uniquely human, complex topics: things like how to navigate a difficult team dynamic or overcome imposter syndrome.[27] We see personalized coaching as more than a perk. It's a strategic investment that helps employees build the skills they need to thrive.' The results: Ninety-seven percent of participants say they feel more confident navigating their careers after coaching.

There's an important step that companies can't skip here, though. Managers themselves need coaching and support. Nearly 80 percent of global CHROs agree that managers in the future will spend less time managing tasks and more time coaching teams.[28] Yet most managers were promoted for their technical expertise, not their coaching ability.

Companies Are Work Charts, Not Org Charts

So, when companies invest in more coaching, they shouldn't forget coaches who can help managers develop their 5Cs. AI tools can help here too. For example, LinkedIn Learning's AI-powered coaching helps managers practice difficult conversations and receive personalized feedback anytime they need to. AI can't do the 5Cs, but it acts as an excellent tool for learning, and as a way to practice those capabilities.

This investment in coaching gets to a deeper truth: Thriving in the AI era means being as committed to your talent as you are to your technology. It means being as pro-human as you are pro-AI. Yes, you need cutting-edge tools, but you also need a cutting-edge culture where people want to stay and grow. As barriers to entrepreneurship fall and new businesses emerge, today's companies are going to have to offer what those other options may not: a culture of collective learning, the scale to work on world-changing problems, and the support systems that help people become their best.

When companies get this right, it creates a ripple effect across the organization. Ideas flow more freely. Hands raise higher. Old assumptions get challenged more frequently. Innovation spreads.

As AI handles the routine work, human creativity and energy become our most critical resources, as vital as code or computing power, but requiring fundamentally different care. Companies who understand this truth will do more than just find the best people. They will create the environment where those people do their best work.

OPEN TO WORK

Small Is Big: The Hidden Advantage

Reading about big companies with big programs, you might be thinking: Easy for them. They have lots of people and big budgets to match. My business is smaller. I have fewer resources, less margin for error. Here's the thing: If you run a small shop, you may have a big opportunity right now. And we should all be rooting for you to seize it.

Small and medium businesses (SMBs) are the backbone of the global economy. In the United States alone, since 2019, small businesses have created over 70 percent of net new jobs.[29] SMBs are the vast majority of businesses worldwide and account for up to 60 to 70 percent of total employment and 50 percent of GDP worldwide.[30] Their impact is especially crucial in emerging markets, where they create seven out of every ten new jobs. Despite this vital role in economic growth and community support, SMBs are too often lacking in conversations about technological change, including the future of AI at work.

That should change. SMBs have a hidden advantage right now precisely because of their size. SMBs already operate with the entrepreneurial mindset crucial for the new economy. Employees wear multiple hats, adapt quickly to market changes, and find creative solutions with limited resources. This flexibility, often born of necessity, is exactly what the AI economy will reward.

As a result, the three shifts we've outlined become far simpler at a smaller scale. Making skills visible doesn't require an expensive platform overhaul, just conversations with your team about hidden talents and untapped potential. Training managers to coach rather than supervise? In a team of fifteen, that's a series of honest discussions, not a corporate-wide initiative. With fewer employees, everything moves faster.

That includes growth for the business too, once you bring AI into the equation.

Talk to any small business owner and they'll likely tell you that one of the biggest barriers to growth is working *in* the business more than working *on* it. By that they mean getting stuck in daily operations rather than thinking about new products, new markets, and new opportunities.

AI tools can help change this equation. For example, AI-driven analytics can help SMBs identify new market trends, customer needs, and potential risks, giving a local business owner insights that once required hiring a team of analysts. Given the cost and difficulties that exist around hiring for SMBs, AI tools can help the people they already have do more sophisticated work.

That all matters because, as the Bureau of Labor Statistics reports, roughly 20 percent of small businesses fail in their first year, and roughly 50 percent fail within five years, often not because the idea was bad but because owners couldn't find the time or resources to grow strategically.[31]

The opportunity for SMBs in this new era is enormous. Research from LinkedIn on small businesses found that 73 percent of small business marketers globally agree AI helps smaller brands compete and punch above their weight.[32]

Additionally, it found that generative AI could unlock $4.1 trillion in U.S. productivity, with small businesses driving up to 40 percent of that.

This brings us back to the innovation explosion. It's not just startups we're talking about there. It's also existing businesses that can suddenly reach new heights. The bakery on Main Street that uses AI to streamline operations and is able to expand to three locations. The local artisan who can now manage global e-commerce and shipping as easily as selling at the farmers market. The real estate broker who spots a new business opportunity one month and is able to launch it the next.

If AI can remove the barriers that often kept small businesses small, from the analytics they couldn't afford to the complexity they couldn't manage to the time trapped in daily operations, we could unlock growth potential that was always there but never truly accessible. Multiply that by millions and millions of SMBs worldwide, and you get innovation at a new scale. That's good for owners, employees, communities, and all of us who benefit from a more dynamic economy.

Just Start

This chapter has covered a lot of ground. That's because there's genuinely a lot for companies to think about and navigate right now. AI touches everything: how you're structured, how you hire, how you develop people, how you compete for talent, how fast you move.

Companies Are Work Charts, Not Org Charts

But perhaps the single most important thing is the idea that you have to start somewhere.

Think of Conor's two major insights here. One, you don't need to be a technologist or technologically savvy to use AI; you just need to talk to it. And two, the people who will understand best how to make AI work in the workplace are the people who are doing the jobs.

Conor notes that giving your employees access to AI tools and encouraging them to use them means that 'you just sort of say, like, hey, listen, solve that problem … You don't have to set people in place anymore. You just have to give them the task and the opportunity of technology to be able to do that.'

If you're leading a team, pick one painful process everyone hates. Pose it as a challenge: Who wants to fix this? Give your team time to think about it and permission to ignore old rules and create something better. The key is that you have to mean it. When that team comes back with an idea that pushes on some established ways of work, you have to back them.

As Séverine Charbon, CHRO at Publicis Groupe, puts it, 'The number one skill you need to master [as an HR leader] is to be able to navigate complexity and ambiguity and constantly adapt to change.'[33]

She's right. And it's not just true for those leading companies. It's also true for those leading economies. Because as workers and companies start adapting, the world we all operate in, the economy itself, also needs to adapt. That's where we're going next.

The Bottom Line

1. **The org chart was built for the past; the work chart is built for the future.** Just as factory owners had to stop treating electricity like a better steam engine, today's companies will not succeed by bolting AI onto existing structures. The shift from org chart to work chart means organizing around the work in entirely new ways.

2. **Three shifts help bring about the work chart.** Leading by design not command, seeing capabilities not just categories, and managing by coaching. When companies get this right, they will create an environment where everyone is able to do their best work.

3. **Small businesses have big advantages when it comes to speed and agility.** They already operate with the entrepreneurialism the age of AI will reward: wearing multiple hats, adapting quickly, finding creative solutions with limited resources.

CHAPTER 8

Economies Need Innovation from All, for All

Kate Kallot calls herself the 'data plumber' for the Global South. 'The whole world is grappling with how they can serve safe water to everybody,' she says. In her metaphor, the 'safe water' is AI models and datasets. 'But right now, the plumbing to do so doesn't exist in Africa. So we built that entire plumbing system.'[1]

In 2022, Kate left her position running Nvidia's emerging markets business in New York to found Amini, a startup in Nairobi building data centers and analytic tools for the African continent. The company deploys locally controlled data infrastructure that enables nations to own and monetize their data, unlocking new pathways for economic growth.

Born in France, Kate frequently visited family in Africa while she was growing up. As an adult, she decided to move to Kenya because she saw something others were missing: Extraordinary AI innovation was already happening across the Global South, but the infrastructure in place wasn't strong enough for the region to become a leader.

OPEN TO WORK

'When you think about what Silicon Valley considers AI breakthroughs today,' Kate says, 'it's mostly new computer infrastructure or new model architecture. But we can't compete on that stage because we don't have the same level of resources. When I think about AI in Africa, the innovation doesn't come from fundamental research. It comes from applied AI and how we're using existing technologies in our context, which is very, very different from the context of the Global North.'

Kate's vision requires partnership from governments. 'Building critical infrastructure today means building your own data infrastructure,' she tells policymakers. 'It's not just another digital divide. It's entire generations that will be left out.'

Governments must create the right ecosystem and infrastructure so that developers can build and apply AI in ways that work for their country. 'It's an opportunity for an interesting switch,' Kate says, 'where, all of a sudden, the value creation economically doesn't just happen in the Global North.'

In March 2025, the Kenyan government launched a national AI strategy, driven in part by founders like Kate.[2] The strategy targets what matters most to the region. One government-backed program focuses on the nation's shortage of doctors: roughly one doctor for every six thousand, rather than the WHO recommendation of one for every thousand people. The result is a large-scale pilot program to determine whether an AI assistant for clinicians can enhance the accuracy of diagnoses, ensure that treatments follow national guidelines, and generally boost the quality of health services. The program aims to bring AI-assisted health care to nine thousand Nairobi patients in the continent's largest trial of its kind.

Kenya is just one example of an economy that isn't waiting for change to happen to it, but is actively shaping how AI transforms work and opportunity. Every economy right now faces this same choice: adapt with intention or be reshaped by accident.

The Disrupted

Right now, around seven hundred million people all over the world, which is equivalent to about 10 percent of humanity, live without electricity.[3] In sub-Saharan Africa, close to 50 percent of people live without access to power. That has many implications for everyday life, including locking all those people out of the modern global economy, which is increasingly computer- and internet-based. As we look to the future, without electricity, there's no access to AI. And without access to AI, there's none of the opportunity we're discussing in this book.

So, access is the first thing that people need in order to be part of the economic growth that's coming. But, as Conor Grennan from NYU said in the previous chapter, people can't just have the tool. They need to use it.

It turns out that the history of how the adoption of electricity impacted economic growth offers important insight into how essential it will be for governments to ensure AI adoption, not just access. That must be front and center in policy plans moving forward.

More than a century ago, inventors across the globe built their first electric power stations within a few years of each other. But it was the United States that figured out how to spread electricity faster than anyone else, into more factories, more homes, and more hands. By 1929, electricity was available in about two-thirds of American homes.[4] Research has shown that widespread access and adoption unleashed a wave of innovation:[5] electric streetcars, pop-up toasters, washing machines. These inventions came to define modern life and helped make America the commercial hub it is today.

The lesson here is that the winners of this new age won't be determined solely by those who build the most sophisticated algorithms, but by those who get AI tools into the most hands most effectively. And so, as Kate advocates, governments will need to make widespread access to and adoption of AI a priority.

In addition, governments need to help the communities set to feel this disruption understand what's coming and how they can manage this moment of big change as it unfolds. Remember the Luddites from chapter 1? They weren't wrong about what technological change meant for them. They suffered enormously, with little to no support to help them adjust. We should all be trying to avoid that happening again, especially given the scale of disruption ahead.

Individuals and organizations can only do so much. Governments must step in, investing in retraining programs and creating new pathways into new types of work. The specific approaches will vary by country and culture, but the imperative to support people, especially those who will feel this disruption first, should not.

Few understand what's coming for economies better than Maria Flynn. As president and CEO of Jobs for the Future (JFF), a nonprofit transforming education and workforce systems in the United States, Maria brings sixteen years of experience from the U.S. Department of Labor. Her vision for how economies should adapt goes back well beyond that, however, to mornings spent in a vocational high school where her mother was the school secretary.[6]

'I was in fourth grade when she took that job,' Maria says. 'Every morning from fourth grade through eighth grade, I would go to her school for an hour before mine started. I got to know the students and the instructors.' There was a stigma attached to these programs: Auto mechanics, cosmetology, and trades were considered backups for students who weren't college-bound. But Maria saw something else. 'These programs are incredible. You wonder, What's the stigma about?'

Today, Maria is pushing for the kind of reform that will change how economies value labor and train workers for what's ahead. 'We're in a perfect storm of change,' she explains. 'The advancements in AI over the past three years are unlike anything anyone anticipated. We're still in the early innings of what's possible. I worry that no one in the ecosystem, from communities to companies to federal programs, is responding fast enough. The need is going to quickly become extremely urgent.'

Maria's right to worry. But the urgency isn't just about responding faster. It's about responding differently, which is something she and JFF are trying to make clear to leaders.

'I hope that we will be an economy that centers skills, that we really are building pathways into quality jobs that really center the skills that individuals have more so than the degrees that they have from any particular institution, and that we are making those pathways both accessible and transparent,' Maria says.

Maria is careful to add that every policy decision must put the real anxiety that people are facing at the center.

'There's all this theoretical conversation around the future of work, but, really, what workers want to know right now is, What's the future of me? What's my future?'

The Economy of the Future

For centuries, economies measured success by efficiency: how much we could produce, how fast, how cheaply. That's what built the industrial world. Now, machines are set to out-efficiency us, which means what matters most for humans at work is what machines can't do. Shoring up that human edge requires creating conditions where entrepreneurial thinking and innovation can flourish in every corner of an economy, not just in elite circles.

It starts with how we teach. The College Board's new AP course Business with Personal Finance gives high school students hands-on entrepreneurial experience. Paul credits his own entrepreneurial success partly to a high school entrepreneurship course, noting that 'most of the population does not have that. And I think that's a critical missing link.'

But this kind of training can't stop at high school. Cross-disciplinary university programs that integrate humanities with technical fields are preparing students to spot opportunities that pure specialists miss. Companies are training employees to identify problems and experiment with solutions rather than just execute tasks. The pattern is clear: Entrepreneurial thinking is a capability that can be developed at any stage. And it must be.

Promoting entrepreneurialism starts in education, for students of all ages. But it doesn't end there. Governments will need to encourage entrepreneurialism at every level of the economy, especially around areas of national interest. Take the example of Singapore. When Singapore set out to make biomedicine one of its main economic pillars, the idea that a tiny island nation could compete with major markets might have seemed overly ambitious.[7] Singapore's rationale was simple: Competitive advantages aren't inherited; they're built. Sometimes literally. A centerpiece of their effort was Biopolis,[8] a research campus for biotechnology and life sciences. It was designed to force collaboration: seven glass buildings connected by sky bridges angled so biologists could peer into engineers' laboratories.

This kind of thinking is spreading. From Tennessee[9] to Texas,[10] Colorado[11] to Pennsylvania,[12] regions in the United States are creating networks where university researchers, businesses, and investors come together through deliberate public-private partnerships. Shared facilities are emerging where government contractors collaborate with commercial firms and academic researchers, with tax incentives helping to strengthen partnerships.

At an individual level, there's still an access issue. Being more entrepreneurial in your job is one thing. Trying to be an entrepreneur as your job is another. It requires taking risks, especially financial risks. Most people can't quit their jobs to chase an idea or tap professional networks they never built.

Expanding access to capital and support for small and medium-sized businesses is critical to unlocking innovation that would otherwise never emerge, let alone scale.

As Paul from MIT puts it: 'As we lower the barriers to entrepreneurship, we increase economic opportunity. And when we do that, all of a sudden you see people creating companies who never would have had the opportunity to do that before. You see people thriving in their jobs who may not have had the opportunity to do so previously.'[13]

The Three Shifts

All of this speaks to the heart of the economy of the future. Teaching entrepreneurial thinking at every level. Building systems that connect sectors and ideas. Creating greater access to the tools that innovation requires. This transformation necessitates deliberate choices about how we structure our economies. And we think three fundamental shifts will determine whether regions thrive or get left behind.

Economies Need Innovation from All, for All

Shift 1: Credentials AND Capabilities

Here's a story that plays out, in some form or another, over and over again in today's world of work: A hiring manager has two candidates. One has a degree from a prestigious university and solid grades. The other doesn't, but has built successful projects, mastered new technology, and solved problems the first candidate has only read about in textbooks.

Who gets hired? Usually, the one with the degree. Not necessarily because they're more capable, but because credentials are easier to verify than capabilities.

That's the system we built in the industrial age, when work was stable and skills lasted decades. A degree signaled, among other things, that you could handle complexity and finish what you started. But in an economy where skills shift constantly and AI democratizes access to knowledge, that system is breaking down.

The classic credentials, from degree to job title, got us here. In a work chart world, they're not enough anymore. That's why economies readying for this new world are building systems that recognize the skills people actually have and the ones they can keep developing as work changes.

Take India. In a country where less than a third of professionals feel prepared to use AI tools, EY and Microsoft launched the AI Skills Passport in 2025.[14] The free online program trains young adults on AI fundamentals and real-world applications. Learners complete hands-on exercises and case studies that prove what they can actually do. When they finish, they earn a verifiable digital badge. It's a credential tied directly to demonstrated capability. The program reached tens of thousands of people in its first year, with plans to extend access to economically disadvantaged youth through nonprofit partnerships.

Kate Kallot put this same approach into practice at Amini, sometimes with surprising results.

When Kate hires, she says, 'We actually look practically at the skills you have, and our interviews are more practical than they are theoretical. In the context we operate, it doesn't matter what degree you have. It's, How are you able to solve problems? And are you able to solve problems in a way that makes sense, that is consistent? And do you actually know some of the technology you have to use for that? How are you able to figure it out, even in a very restricted environment? Oftentimes, African developers come [out] on top of other developers, because figuring it out is all that they've had to do.'

Recently, one of her top performers on Amini's technical team, who doesn't have a computer science degree, was interviewing candidates for a job.

'He interviewed someone who was coming from Google, and he looks at me and is like, Kate, on paper, he's great, you know? But I realized that he's never built a website by himself. Front-end developers at Google, they just have to maintain one small thing. How is he going to make it here? When you have to change everything … he's not going to be able to survive.'

In rural Karnataka, India, the nonprofit Karya has taken a similar approach, focusing on hiring for capabilities workers

Economies Need Innovation from All, for All

have, including those they have sharpened in their everyday life. Karya pays rural Indians above minimum wage to help make AI work not just for widely spoken languages like English and Mandarin, but also for regional Indian languages like Kannada, Marathi, Telugu, Hindi, Bengali, and Malayalam.[15]

With Karya, workers record themselves speaking in their native dialect, transcribe conversations with attention to regional expressions, and evaluate whether an AI's response makes cultural sense in their community. By doing that, they're teaching computers to understand the everyday speech patterns, local idioms, and cultural nuances that define communication at a local level. Their capability doesn't come from a degree or a title. It's the mother tongue they've carried their whole lives paired with the ability to use that knowledge to train AI.

As co-founder Vivek Seshadri puts it, 'As people were getting access to smartphones, we asked if there was productive work they could do.'[16] The answer was yes. More significantly, every time a person engages in this 'dignified digital work,' they're learning to interact with the digital economy while contributing capabilities that wouldn't be captured by traditional credential systems.

This approach recognizes that the most valuable skills in an AI economy aren't simply technical. The 5Cs and the entrepreneurialism that comes from them become essential capabilities. These uniquely human skills can't be easily credentialed, but they can be recognized, developed, and valued.

The case for bringing capabilities into the mix is compelling. LinkedIn's data shows that skills-based hiring could expand the talent pool by an average of six times compared to traditional credential requirements.[17] For economies facing labor shortages, this shift will soon be a mathematical necessity.

Former Italian prime minister Mario Draghi's recent report on European competitiveness calls for creating a continental 'skills-based' economy: a 'Union of Skills' where businesses and governments care about what people can actually do, not where they went to school.[18] 'The emphasis shifts from the formal delivery of diplomas to preparing students with the right skills,' Draghi writes.

The most powerful signal comes when governments practice what they preach. A few years ago, the U.S. federal government told agencies to stop requiring college degrees for jobs that don't legally need them, opening thousands of federal jobs to people who'd been locked out.[19]

Maryland became the first state to eliminate degree requirements for most positions, instantly making more than half of its thirty-eight thousand government jobs accessible to candidates without bachelor's degrees.[20] Utah eliminated degree requirements for 98 percent of state positions.[21] Twenty other states have followed suit. When the largest employer in most places, the government, starts valuing capabilities, it signals change throughout the economy.[22]

Shift 2: Foundational Learning AND Lifelong Learning

Workers know something education systems don't always account for: One degree isn't enough to last a lifetime. Jobs shift too fast. New tools arrive too quickly. People are left scrambling to keep up, signing up for AI courses, teaching themselves skills on the fly, doing whatever it takes to stay employable. At LinkedIn, we've seen nearly a 170 percent surge in non-tech professionals enrolling in AI courses. Our members are showing us, in real time, that they're hungry to learn and adapt at all stages of their career.

Of course, individual hustle can only go so far. Without infrastructure designed for lifelong learning, or education that's flexible, continuous, and tied directly to work, workers are climbing a wall with few footholds.

Traditional higher education is built around the idea that learning is basically a onetime event. You go to college at eighteen, maybe add grad school in your twenties, and by thirty your education is pretty much over. If you weren't ready at the 'right' age, or if life got in the way, too bad. The system quietly signals to millions they've missed their chance.

Maria Anguiano has been trying to change that.[23] At Arizona State University (ASU), she built the Learning Enterprise to help people keep learning their whole lives. The initiative intentionally expands opportunity for nontraditional students, from working adults to career changers.

OPEN TO WORK

'Different people are ready for different challenges at different parts of their life,' she explains. 'If you haven't figured life out, or if you're not really good at school, by the time you're eighteen, you've lost all these opportunities.'

For Anguiano, this idea is personal. At her California high school, fewer than 10 percent of her graduating class attended a four-year college. 'It worked for me,' she says with irony, 'but it didn't work for the majority of the kids I went to high school with.'

Her solution is breaking education into digestible, stackable pieces. 'We had a new master of science in artificial intelligence in business, but we also broke it down in a modular way. You could take the first three months as just a standalone certificate. If you want to continue, great. You already have three months' worth. If not, you got three months of education.'

To date, ASU's Learning Enterprise has served more than 1.2 million learners globally.[24] Nearly nine thousand adult learners have been admitted. Over one million have upskilled or reskilled through career and professional learning courses.

Another example of this thinking is Western Governors University (WGU), which has built an entire institution around working adults navigating career transitions.

Founded in 1997 by nineteen governors who understood that geographic barriers and rigid schedules were keeping millions from accessing education, WGU has pioneered competency-based learning at scale.[25] Progress isn't measured by hours in a classroom but by demonstrating mastery of actual skills. Every student works with a dedicated mentor

Economies Need Innovation from All, for All

who understands that a thirty-five-year-old switching from retail to data analytics needs different support than an eighteen-year-old freshman.

There's urgency to scaling this approach. The Organisation for Economic Co-operation and Development (OECD) looks at how economies are doing when it comes to creating opportunity. In 2023, they found that participation in adult education is 'stagnating or even declining in many countries,' and when gaps between socioeconomic groups narrow, it's often because higher-skilled workers are dropping out, not because low-income groups are being reached. Single parents and factory workers remain underserved in most major economies.[26]

The finding makes it pretty clear that governments need to help create flexible, accessible education that meets people where they are, whether that's a parent taking online courses at night or a factory worker learning AI basics during lunch breaks.

Educational institutions also need to shift what they teach, not just how. For decades, a chapter like this would have emphasized STEM skills. While those remain vital, what we need in the AI era is the know-how behind human innovation. That means teaching and credentialing the 5Cs and entrepreneurialism as deliberately as we once taught engineering or computer science.

How do we do that? One possible entry point is redesigning to the humanities, which are natural teachers of the 5Cs. We just need to highlight their applicability. We've seen this story before. Mathematics was once considered largely theoretical until the industrial age made it essential for engineering. The humanities now face a similar inflection point. Literature, philosophy, and history have been cultivating critical thinking, ethical reasoning, and empathy for centuries. Those capabilities, once treated as peripheral, are about to become as central to the AI economy as mathematics became to the industrial one.

Shift 3: Public Leadership AND Private Partnership

The first two shifts aren't optional upgrades. They're essential transformations. Importantly, no single entity can make them happen alone. Not governments. Not companies. Not educational institutions. The only way forward is through deliberate collaboration across sectors.

This collaboration must focus on two interconnected challenges: ensuring AI access through infrastructure and enabling AI adoption through education and training.

For infrastructure, the scale of private capital investment is unprecedented. In 2025 alone, Microsoft, Google, Amazon, and Nvidia announced investments of tens of billions of dollars to expand data centers, develop semiconductors, and build high-performance AI computing networks.[27] As Kate's work in Kenya demonstrates, this infrastructure investment must reach beyond traditional tech hubs. Without deliberate effort to build AI infrastructure in the Global South, we risk creating a new digital divide: one that locks entire regions out of the AI economy before it even begins.

Economies Need Innovation from All, for All

In education, we're seeing progress too. Microsoft's 2025 commitment[28] is a good example, representing a multibillion-dollar pledge to train twenty million people in AI skills, partnering with community colleges, K-12 schools, and nonprofits. The initiative recognizes a shared reality: Companies need educational institutions to develop pipelines of talent, schools need industry partnerships to stay current, and workers need both sectors collaborating to create legitimate paths for continuous reskilling.

Another example is the partnership between tech companies and the American Federation of Teachers (AFT). In 2025, Microsoft, OpenAI, and Anthropic committed millions to create the National Academy for AI Instruction in Manhattan, which is a new model for how technology companies, labor organizations, and educational institutions can work together In early 2025.[29]

The partnership addresses a fundamental tension. Teachers across America are watching AI transform their classrooms in real time as students use ChatGPT for homework, administrators push AI tools, and parents worry about what the development of AI means for their children. Meanwhile, tech companies are building educational AI tools at breakneck speed, often without understanding classroom realities, and unions are advocating to make sure their members aren't replaced by the technology they're being asked to embrace.

Rather than letting these forces pull in opposite directions, the academy brings them together. It will provide free AI training to nearly two million AFT members, aiming to reach four hundred thousand educators in the first five years.[30] As AFT president Randi Weingarten puts it, 'Teachers must be in charge of education – not the tool, not the machine.'[31]

Educators learn practical applications like creating lesson plans and quizzes with AI, but they also provide feedback that shapes how these tools develop.

So, the union brings expertise about classroom realities. The tech companies bring cutting-edge tools and technical knowledge. Together, they're building something neither could create alone: technology not *for* educators but *with* them.

This kind of cross-sector partnership is really the only way to navigate this moment. No company can retrain an entire economy's workforce alone. No government can legislate its way to inclusive innovation. No union can protect jobs that are fundamentally changing. Together, though, they can build a new world of work that creates more opportunity for workers, not less.

Leaders Who Get It

The difference between economies that will succeed and those that will fall behind likely comes down to leadership that understands what communities need to make it through this transformation.

Picture a mayor who visits the local community college to see what types of training actually lead to jobs. A governor who spends time with laid-off workers figuring out what support would help them get back on their feet, whether with a new job or business. A cabinet minister who experiments with AI tools not because staff told them to, but because they're genuinely curious about how these technologies might help constituents. These are leaders who feel this change in their bones; who understand what's at stake not just in reports but in daily life.

The work ahead for policymakers is unprecedented as economies adapt in ways that hopefully lead to greater innovation and access. That's why your voice and vote matter more than ever.

When choosing leaders at any level, ask, Do they understand the workforce implications of AI beyond talking points? Have they shown genuine commitment to helping people manage economic disruption? Are they investing in infrastructure that builds innovation capacity? Can they balance efficiency with entrepreneurship?

The governments that succeed in the age of AI won't be the ones with the best ideas on paper. They'll be the ones that actually build the programs and support that people need.

So advocate for a more focused conversation on the future of work. Look for leaders who understand that this transition requires investment in people, not just platforms. But while you're pushing for systems to change, remember: You have agency too.

Throughout this book, we've examined jobs, careers, companies, and economies. We've shown you the big patterns reshaping the world of work.

OPEN TO WORK

Now we turn to you. Not as an employee or worker, but as a human and individual. Because, as we've pointed out along the way, in the age of AI, your uniqueness is going to become your sturdiest competitive advantage. The next section is about understanding what makes you irreplaceable and how to start writing your own story into the future of work.

The Bottom Line

1. **The economies that pull ahead won't just be the ones that invent AI; they'll be the ones that make widespread adoption possible.** Just as America's dominance in the electrical age came from getting electricity into more hands, the age of AI belongs to regions that make the technology commonplace. Access and adoption are what determine winners.

2. **Three shifts are essential for economies.** Value credentials *and* capabilities, foundational education *and* lifelong-learning, public leadership *and* private partnership. These shifts are already underway, with organizations like Microsoft and the AFT showing what's possible.

3. **Leaders who get it will set their communities up to succeed in this new era.** The disruption is here. The leaders who get that understand that support and new thinking are needed now, not later. They understand navigating this transformation requires more than simply an investment in platforms. It demands an investment in people.

PART III
THE PATH FORWARD

CHAPTER 9

Nobody Beats You at Being You

There are well over three billion people in the global workforce. More than a billion of them are on LinkedIn. Only one of them is you.

That might sound obvious, but it's easy to forget when you're at work, trying to fit in. We often spend our careers molding ourselves to job descriptions, to industry standards, to the 'proven path.' We're asked to demonstrate the right competencies so we can show that we can do what others have already done. The entire machinery of work, from résumés to reviews, is designed to make us comparable, categorizable, and measurable against others. And for good reason: That's how the industrial age worked. Standardization was the point.

When AI handles the standard, though, things start to flip. Suddenly your differences aren't limitations. They're your competitive advantage.

Think about what that actually means. The specific combination of failures and triumphs that taught you resilience in ways no curriculum could capture. The childhood spent between cultures that lets you see patterns others miss. The decade you 'wasted' in the wrong career that gave you insights no straight path could provide. The quirks in how you approach problems. The unconventional connections you make between ideas.

For your entire career, you've probably been told to smooth over these edges; to make yourself more marketable, more comparable to others in your field. In a world where AI can replicate the standard approach, those edges are going to become what make you irreplaceable.

Consider how this plays out in practice. When you defined your career in chapter 6 through *why*, *what*, and *where*, you weren't trying to match someone else's path. You were claiming your own. That's not an accident. When you build from what's natural to you, you're not competing with everyone who has similar credentials. You're competing with nobody, because nobody else has your exact mix.

The entrepreneur Naval Ravikant captured this perfectly in an interview: 'The more you do things that are natural to you, the less competition you have … No one is going to beat you at being you.'[1]

Throughout this book, we've shared the view we have as the world's largest network of professionals: how jobs are breaking into tasks, how careers are becoming like climbing walls, how the skills that matter are shifting beneath our feet.

But all that data can't tell us your story. And honestly? Your story is the one that matters most.

We've found that sometimes one person's unconventional path lights the spark someone else needs to reimagine their own future. So before we get to the practical tool kit in the next chapter, we want to focus on something more fundamental: What makes you *you*? Not in some abstract way, but in the specific, irreplaceable way that becomes your advantage in this new era.

Throughout this chapter, we'll share conversations from *The Path*, a LinkedIn podcast Ryan hosts with leaders who've wrestled with these same questions, leaders who've figured out how to define who they are and build extraordinary careers based on that understanding.

We're going to start with a business leader who created an entire framework for this: the concept of 'onlyness.'

Onlyness

The management thinker Nilofer Merchant coined the term 'onlyness' in an article for the *Harvard Business Review*, then expanded on her theory in two subsequent books.[2]

The definition of onlyness is simple. It's the distinct point of view that each of us has. It's the way we each add value. That point of view is created by your singular life experiences, perspectives, and aspirations. 'We each stand in a spot in the world only one stands in,' Nilofer says. 'It's a function of our distinct history and experience, visions and hopes.'[3]

Nilofer is careful to point out that onlyness isn't about self-help. It's about economic opportunity, especially in the age of AI. She draws on her career in tech and consulting to back this up.

OPEN TO WORK

Once, Nilofer was working with a team of bankers. A member of the team came up to Nilofer after a presentation and explained an idea she had about how to serve the 'underbanked,' which is a term used to describe individuals who tend not to use banks and instead deal in cash, which means they often cash checks, usually for very high fees, instead of depositing them.

The team member, who came from a low-income background herself and had firsthand experience with being underbanked, had an idea about how to serve that community in ways that would still be profitable for the bank. Nilofer and the team member were standing in the corner of the room as others gathered their belongings.

Nilofer recognized the value of the team member's idea, then gestured to her colleagues and said, 'Well, when are you going to tell all these people? We could go make it happen, you know. This is a bank. You guys can solve it and hold a new advantage in the marketplace.'

But, Nilofer says, 'The banker said, "Oh, no, no, I would never tell these people." And I remember the emphasis on *these people*. And then she looked at her colleagues, and she said to me, "Well, that person's wearing an Hermès tie, and that person's carrying a YSL bag." She pointed out all the markers of socioeconomic status that were in the room. And then basically said, I don't want to admit that the reason I know this market is because of my onlyness.

'She was basically saying I should be ashamed, given this room. And I said, Actually, no, you should be celebrating that perspective that only you have, because that is the engine of all innovation. It's not that you do it all by yourself, but you see something that no one else sees. You turn to your colleagues and say, Let me tell you something that you don't see that I do. And then together we can figure out how to go build something new.'

Nilofer didn't develop the idea of onlyness simply by seeing the way it played out in other people's lives. For her, onlyness is personal, tracing back to when she was a nineteen-year-old community college student who had deferred entrance to UC Berkeley because her family couldn't afford to send her there. She was a little anxious at being a community college student, envious of her peers from high school who had gone to four-year colleges. Until, that is, she was asked to become a student board member on a committee founded by California's governor to reform the state's community colleges.

'Up to that point, attending community college had been a negative in my mind. I thought it made me less than those high school friends who had gone off to Harvard, MIT, or UC Berkeley,' Nilofer writes in her book *The Power of Onlyness*. 'Yet this particular experience turned out to be the key to my unique contribution … It's not the "perfection" of your experience that prepares you or earns you a seat at the table but rather simply what you can contribute.'[4]

Her lesson: 'Bring what you distinctly have, align with others who share your purpose, and make it happen, together.'[5]

Nilofer developed this vision well before AI entered the mainstream, but it's even more relevant now. As AI commoditizes technical skills, your edge lies in your singular experiences, unique judgment, empathy, resilience, and problem-solving. Machines can replicate tasks, but they can't replicate you.

OPEN TO WORK

The Power of Your Past

Meet John Henry,[6] a man in his thirties, a born and bred New Yorker with an easy smile whose path to success was anything but easy. His career contains an important lesson for defining onlyness in the age of AI. John's story makes clear that we shouldn't think of our past experiences simply as baggage. Our past experiences are often the best fuel for innovation.

John was born to immigrant parents from the Dominican Republic. His mother worked as a janitor in public schools and his father was a presser at a dry cleaner. After high school, John got a job as a doorman in Manhattan to support himself through community college. He had dreams of going into business and leaving his working-class background behind.

One tenant in the building took John under his wing. The owner of a dry cleaning business, he saw something in the young doorman. John had grown up watching his father work in dry cleaning, knowledge he'd never been particularly proud of until now, when it suddenly mattered. To this mentor, John wasn't just another kid with potential. He was someone who understood the business.

John started working for him while developing his own side hustle: going door-to-door offering a wash-and-fold service. He'd collect laundry, clean it at his mentor's facility, and deliver it back.

Things changed when he got fired from his job as a doorman. He was devastated, but he decided to take it as a sign. Now, he had to focus on his side hustle. Every day he suited up, and from nine to five he went to work collecting, washing, and delivering laundry.

His breakthrough came when he discovered an untapped niche: servicing film sets in New York. Productions needed someone reliable to keep their large volume of costumes clean. John became that someone.

Through a connection from his old doorman job, he had an opportunity to become the dry cleaner for the set of *The Wolf of Wall Street*. 'I picked up the clothes and … I actually took them to my dad,' John says, noting that he usually brought clothes to his mentor's dry-cleaning business to be cleaned. But not this time.

'It was just a moment that was very emotional for me,' John continues, 'because my pops was a presser all growing up, and I was always embarrassed of that, and yet here I am in the most important moment of my career and life so far, and I brought them to my dad. And my dad is a master presser. He pressed those garments really beautifully, and I brought those garments, and he delivered them with me, to *The Wolf of Wall Street*, and they were like, This is amazing, you get the whole account, and by the way, there's a new account in town, and if you get them, you're going to be okay for a long time. And that was *Law and Order* … We ended up cornering, dominating, film and television, all the wardrobe, as a nineteen-year-old kid with no formal experience.'

What John had long thought was a disadvantage was also his advantage. John's father had a valuable skill. On the most important day of John's career, John was able to fully appreciate this. At the time, he was nineteen years old. Two years later he sold his dry-cleaning business for a million dollars.

John went on to launch businesses that intentionally give back to his community: an incubator in Harlem and a car insurance startup meant to work against bias in the industry. And he also went on to host podcasts and a TV show, and then joined an investment firm. His goal was not just to succeed as only he could, but to help others do the same.

The Power of Being First

It may seem like a disadvantage to be an outsider, but Leena Nair is a leader[7] whose career demonstrates how being a newcomer can become your greatest strategic advantage.

Leena is currently the global CEO of Chanel, the French luxury brand. When we had her on *The Path*, she shared that she grew up in a small Indian town where girls rarely had careers. At eight, she stood in front of many of her classmates and announced that she wanted to be prime minister. Her classmates laughed, but that declaration set a pattern: Leena would spend her life pushing back against assumptions of what she could be or not be.

When she got a job at Unilever, as part of their prestigious management program, she embraced her outsider status and turned it into something no one else could replicate. 'I remember in many ways the privilege and responsibility of being the first,' she says. 'I was the first woman to go into a factory. I was the first woman to do a night shift. I was the first woman to do one of the difficult jobs in the south of India.'

Rather than minimizing her differences, she leveraged them. Leena had always had to decode unwritten rules and study systems that weren't second nature to her, so she developed an emotional intelligence others didn't. She could spot when talented people were being inadvertently excluded. She knew what it felt like to defy expectations. As a result, she could help others do the same.

'One thing I realized very early on in my career was that I truly liked to look at business through the lens of the people who worked in it,' she says. 'I felt more and more that my purpose was to ignite the spark in others so that people who came to me would feel like the possibilities were endless. They could do anything. They could create magic.'

This approach took Leena from engineering graduate to Unilever's first female CHRO, overseeing more than a hundred thousand employees. Then came the call that changed everything: Chanel wanted her as CEO.

'I had self-doubts,' she admits. But she understood something crucial: 'The fundamentals of a good business, the principles of good leadership are transferable across sectors.'

And there was one other thing. Chanel's founder, Gabrielle Chanel, had also been an outsider. She had spent her adolescence in an orphanage after her mother died, and it was there that she learned to sew. She disrupted fashion precisely because she saw it differently.

'The story of our legendary founder, Gabrielle Chanel, was a radical innovator. So I loved being able to walk in her footsteps and get inspired by her,' Leena says.

Leena's outsider lens wasn't a liability. It was exactly what the role required. Nobody else could be her.

The Power of Speaking Your Mind

In a world where AI can generate perfect, polished responses, Scott Galloway's success shows us why speaking your mind, even when what you have to say is a little bit messy, can be your greatest advantage. Now in his early sixties, the NYU professor, entrepreneur, and prolific podcaster has built his career on saying what others won't, but his journey to radical authenticity wasn't immediate.[8]

Scott started his life without privilege. Born to a single mother who worked as a secretary in Los Angeles, he scraped through UCLA and Berkeley before launching companies. Some were spectacular successes, others expensive lessons in humility.

Scott's breakthrough came when he stopped hiding his failures and developed the courage to speak about them publicly. His personal setbacks, his business setbacks, the times he was fired. Instead of burying these experiences, he turned them into his competitive advantage: He had earned the right to tell hard truths because he'd lived them.

'The key to my success was rejection,' he says, 'specifically my ability to endure it.'

That credibility, built from real experience, not theoretical knowledge, is what makes his provocations land differently than others'. While others in academia remained diplomatic, even silent, Scott would criticize his own industry. He called universities 'luxury brands' that don't always have students' interests at heart. When it comes to business, he provocatively stated, 'Brand is dead,' challenging widely held marketing beliefs and angering peers who then publicly rebutted his opinions. The point here is about the debate, the idea of launching conversations others are afraid to start, for the sake of refining and challenging deeply held beliefs in business and beyond.

His willingness to voice new opinions, rooted in his specific experiences of struggle and failure, became exactly what made him irreplaceable. In an age of curated content and AI-generated polish, Scott brings his full, complicated humanity to everything he does. And that's precisely why millions listen to him.

He doesn't try to be anyone else. He can't be replicated. And that's the point.

The Power of Being the Underdog

'You'll never succeed without me.'[9] That's what Barbara Corcoran's boyfriend told her when he left her for her secretary and kicked her out of their real estate business. He was wrong.

Barbara, who is now a judge on *Shark Tank*, went on to build the Corcoran Group into a $66 million real estate empire. While she did, she proved that being underestimated isn't a weakness. It's fuel.

'I knew I was going to be successful just to prove him wrong,' Barbara says of that boyfriend. 'I knew I would die rather than let him see me fall on my face.'

Barbara's story shows how rejection and being the 'little guy' can become the foundation of your onlyness.

Barbara grew up in a working-class family, one of ten children raised by a fearless mother. She worked twenty-two jobs by age twenty-three, from playground supervisor to hot dog vendor. In that time, she discovered two gifts that would help define her onlyness: 'I was good at talking, not writing. I could talk a dog off a meat wagon in any job I had. And I also learned that I had a great imagination,' she said when we had her on *The Path*.

After her boyfriend left her, Barbara started the Corcoran Group from scratch with seven agents. It was then that Barbara noticed something about her competition. 'Every business was owned by … a second- or third-generation wealthy kid … The minute I sensed they were cocky, I knew I was coming to get him.'

She called their weakness 'false confidence' and used her underdog status as a weapon. 'I had nothing to lose. I had everything to gain. I threw everything at the wall and a lot of stuff worked.' While established firms coasted on reputation, Barbara reimagined real estate marketing. She launched trend reports, used high-quality photos, created neighborhood guides, and personalized every property story.

Nobody Beats You at Being You

Her approach to building talent reflected her onlyness too. Like Leena, she possessed the emotional intelligence of someone who had had to struggle to achieve. 'I could see the light in you that you couldn't see in yourself, much like my mother saw it in us.' This created fierce loyalty. No one left her company in twelve years unless she fired them.

Even after selling the Corcoran Group for millions,[10] Barbara kept leveraging her scrappy outsider perspective. When *Shark Tank* initially rejected her as a judge, she fired off an email to the executive producer: 'I consider your rejection a lucky charm. Everything good happens to me after I get rejected.' She listed every time someone underestimated her and how she proved them wrong. It worked.

Barbara sums up her philosophy like this. 'I'm never worried about who's competing with me right to the left,' she says. 'I'm always looking behind me, worried about the little guy. And it's really true that the little guy always has the advantage over the big guy in bad times.'

Nilofer, John, Leena, Scott, and Barbara have experienced something AI can never experience: how the messy, complicated, entirely human parts of our journeys can become not bugs to be fixed but features to be celebrated. AI can never know what it's like to realize that the past you were previously ashamed of is actually priceless knowledge. AI can never know how to turn the anxiety of being the first into the confidence to help others be the same. AI can never know what it's like to speak about the difficulty of failure with honesty and humor. AI can never understand the resilience needed to come up from behind when everyone is doubting you.

How Will You Use Your Onlyness?

As Nilofer puts it, 'AI can't imagine a future other than what is already coded. Imagination is one of human beings' greatest gifts. We create. We know how to create a future that doesn't exist today. And so we ought to own that.'[11]

So how do you find your onlyness? Nilofer offers these two exercises to help you on your way.

1. List five stories that have really formed and informed who you are. Then ask yourself, What does that mean for me? What decisions have I made as a result of that?
2. If you were in a Disney movie and found a magic wand that could solve anything, what would you fix?

Nilofer says that there is almost always a throughline here. The first question is about what brings you to today, and the second points to what you'd like to become. She notes that sometimes people stumble with the second question, though, because no one has ever asked them something like it, but she emphasizes that almost everyone has at least one thing they would do with that magic wand.

'We just have to give ourselves permission to just say the thing. However audacious it is, just say the thing. And then once you do, you get to have more strength and capability,' she says.

Your onlyness isn't your résumé. It's the thread that connects your seemingly unrelated experiences into a story only you could have lived. Start with the intersections. Where have you stood at the crossroads of different worlds? What bridges have you built between communities, industries, ways of thinking? What problems do you see that others miss because they haven't walked in your shoes? These intersection points where your unique combination of experiences creates insight no one else has are where your onlyness lives.

Then practice using it. Allow it to inform you as you notice what needs doing and fixing. In meetings, when you offer a perspective, let it come from your onlyness. When mentoring someone, explain not just what to do but why your particular journey led you to that approach. When networking, lead with the problems you're passionate about solving, not the title on your business card.

AI can help here too. Use it to identify patterns in your experiences you might miss. Feed it your career history, your challenges, your victories, and ask it to spot themes. It's not doing your thinking for you. It's acting as an observer, capturing a point of view you might be too close to see.

In the age of AI, recognizing that everyone has an onlyness isn't just poetic. It's practical. When you truly understand that each person you work with, work under, or lead carries their own onlyness, you stop trying to manage everyone the same. You start managing everyone as a distinct individual.

And when you apply this understanding to yourself, when you stop apologizing for your complicated path and start mining it for insight, you discover something big. The very experiences you've been taught to minimize or hide are often your greatest professional assets. The presser's son who expanded an industry. The first woman on a factory floor who saw how to develop talent others missed. The rejected entrepreneur who became a truth-teller. The outsider real estate entrepreneur who had a scrappiness her competitors could only dream of.

Every day, you live an onlyness that no algorithm can replicate or replace. The question isn't whether you have a distinct value; it's whether you'll have the courage to discover it, articulate it, and deploy it. Remember Vivienne Ming's words: 'Everyone is amazing.'

In It Together

When you first opened this book you likely felt a little bit of what the Apollo 13 astronauts experienced, staring at those warning lights. The explosion had happened. AI was transforming work. Familiar systems were failing. At the start of this book, we said we wanted to help you find your footing, discover your edge, and write your story into the future of work.

Hopefully that's all started to happen along the way. And, we hope, something as important has taken hold in your mind too: the fact that you're not alone.

Right now, billions of professionals all over the world are reimagining work together. In that sense, this is an Apollo 13 moment in a way that goes beyond managing disruption.

Years after the mission, in the documentary *Apollo 13: Survival*, Jack Swigert reflected: 'You know, a lot of people ask, "Do you feel that Apollo 13 was a failure?" I guess if you measure success and failure on the basis of, "Did you accomplish what you started out to do?", Apollo 13 was indeed a failure. But Apollo 13 did something that's never happened before in the history of man. That, for a brief instant of time, the whole world was together. Offers of help and messages of concern came from every country in the world. And maybe if you measure Apollo 13, and it is possible for the world to live together, then Apollo 13 was most eminently successful.'[12]

The journey ahead at work is about us as humans and as humankind. Each of us must walk it ourselves, yet none of us will walk alone. It's onlyness at scale. Billions of people defining their particular vision in a world being remade by AI.

The industrial age rewarded efficiency. The AI age will reward entrepreneurialism. Big change is coming, but it's revealing an equally big truth: Much of the work world we're leaving behind isn't worth defending. That doesn't ease the pain of disruption, but it means we can do more than survive. We can succeed by doubling down on the 5Cs: curiosity, courage, creativity, compassion, and communication. These make us irreplaceable. These make us unbeatable.

In the next chapter, we'll walk through concrete steps to navigate what comes next, the tools to use, how to reframe jobs and careers, how to identify and develop your uniquely human capabilities.

Remember, there's only one you. And nothing, not even AI, can beat you at being you.

CHAPTER 10

Open to Work

There's not one set road map that will make sense for everyone, but there are some common starting points we know will set people up for success no matter their role, industry, or level of experience. To give you something concrete to work with, we've tried to distill this book into a 30-60-90-day plan, drawn from all we've learned from over a billion people on LinkedIn, many of whom are already navigating this shift with you. Let's begin.

Days 1–30: AI Foundations

The first step, especially into a new world of work, is often the hardest. You're already ahead there, having read this book and come to it with a decision to act. As you get going, remember that it's okay to pause, restart, or change direction. The key is just to keep moving.

OPEN TO WORK

This first month is about a few foundational things: getting started with AI, knowing where you stand at work with AI, and connecting with people on the same journey.

Getting Started with AI

The best way to learn about AI tools is to find a way back to that same mindset you had as a kid in your favorite class. That moment when you first lit up about your favorite subject, or read the first few pages of the book that sent you down a deeper path of discovery. Try to bring that same curiosity and energy to exploring AI tools and getting started with them.

EXERCISE:
- **Pick one repetitive task you do daily that you often push off to the end of the day.** Maybe it's because it's time-consuming or maybe it's because you just dread doing it. It can be work-related or personal, like writing emails, summarizing documents, creating reports, or even meal or exercise planning for the week.
- **Ask a few trusted colleagues or friends their favorite AI tools** (like Copilot, ChatGPT, Gemini, or Claude) to see what works best for that type of work. There are more people out there than you realize who have been in your shoes and can give you tried-and-true advice on what helped them get started.
- **Find an AI course.** Once you've gotten some trusted input on which tool you're going to explore, try taking

a course on prompting or basic AI fundamentals to get advice on how to frame up the task in a way that an AI tool will easily understand. (There are lots of great, free AI courses out there, including many on LinkedIn Learning.)

- **Get to work on your prompt.** Go back to that repetitive task you identified. Think through all the different pieces of your prompt the same way you would think about communicating context and specific asks to another person you were hiring to help you figure out that task. You can try giving your AI tool a persona to have in mind ('Imagine you're a senior manager at my company'), background on who the audience is ('Preparing a presentation for my marketing peers'), and context on what the goals of the project are ('To convince them to invest in this potential growth opportunity'). If you're striking out on your first few attempts, try rephrasing your prompt with more context or even breaking the task up into smaller steps. Try one new prompt a day.
- **Don't get discouraged.** A note on these early days: You're going to have some false starts. You'll spend twenty minutes crafting what feels like the perfect prompt only to get back something that is totally unhelpful or unusable. You'll try to automate something that turns out to be more complicated than you thought. You'll feel silly asking your AI tool basic questions. This is all completely normal. It's not a sign you're doing it wrong; it's a sign you're actually doing it. You're

not going to master AI in two weeks, but you can get comfortable experimenting. Keep going.

Example: Neil's a consultant who got curious about whether AI could help him as he developed presentations for different clients. He spent some time testing out different tools, and fairly quickly realized that while AI couldn't replicate his deep relationship-building skills, it could help him walk into any conversation more prepared. He taught himself how to construct specific prompts that help him get the best answers: Neil clearly states what he's trying to accomplish up front and shares his initial plans, and then asks AI to point out new ideas or angles he may have missed. He even asks it to offer recommendations from the perspective of an organization development professional or a CEO depending on the meeting he's heading into. He says working with AI 'triggered all kinds of new thinking for me,' and is helping him get done in a few hours what used to take a week.

Knowing Where You Stand

AI will require us to change how we think about our jobs. Instead of seeing your job as one monolithic thing defined by a title, start seeing it as a collection of distinct tasks that will change over time. Some tasks are already better suited for AI to handle, ready to free you up to focus on the tasks that only you can do as a human. The three-bucket framework helps you see this clearly: which tasks to hand off, which to do with AI as your partner, and which are uniquely yours. This shift from 'what is my job?' to 'what are my tasks?' is the key thing to understand.

EXERCISE:
- **List out your top twelve daily or weekly tasks.**
- **Bucket each task into one of three categories:**
  - *Bucket 1:* Tasks AI can do alone (e.g. routine reports, data entry, scheduling)
  - *Bucket 2:* Tasks you do with AI tools (e.g. strategic analysis with AI insights, creative work with AI as partner)
  - *Bucket 3:* Uniquely human tasks (e.g. building trust, making ethical decisions, reading the room)
- **Now, step back and see where you stand across your buckets.** If you aren't sure where a task should be bucketed, go back to chapter 5 for a quick refresher. Ask yourself, Would this task require understanding unspoken context, building trust, or making a judgment call based on values? If yes, it's likely Bucket 3. If it's complex work that benefits from both your expertise and AI's capabilities, it's Bucket 2, where you and AI work best together. If it follows clear rules and patterns, it's probably Bucket 1.
- **Assess your vulnerability.** Calculate what percentage of your time goes to each bucket. If more than half your tasks are in Bucket 1, you're vulnerable for real disruption soon: It's time to either look for new

opportunities or find projects in your current workplace that let you expand beyond your current work. If Bucket 2 is nearly empty, you're missing the chance to use AI as a tool: Start experimenting with AI this week on at least one routine task. If Bucket 3 is less than half your work, you need more time building irreplaceable human skills: Look for opportunities to take on projects involving things like relationship-building or collaborative problem-solving.

- **Restructure your time based on what you learned.** Identify which Bucket 1 tasks you can automate or delegate first, then redirect that time to Bucket 2 and 3 work. The sooner you shift your workday toward using AI tools and adding in uniquely human tasks, the more resilient you'll be.

Example: Taj graduated from a coding bootcamp and has built apps for startups. Like many developers, he realized AI tools can handle much of what fills his day: translating ideas into code, debugging systems, shipping features. These tasks sit in Buckets 1 and 2. After reflection, he saw untapped abilities in Bucket 3: He's a community builder with deep knowledge of his Caribbean neighborhood. Those capabilities led him to build ListedB, a barbershop platform where he focuses on what only he can do while AI handles the routine coding.

Connecting with People on the Journey

When you're feeling frustrated or unsure what to do, please remember this: You are not alone. Far from it. There are hundreds of millions of people just like you facing this moment of change with similar fears and uncertainties. We see it everyday on LinkedIn. Our research shows that over half of the workforce say mastering AI feels like a second job.[1] Posts about feeling overwhelmed while navigating change spiked 56 percent globally in 2025. Importantly, when it comes to big career moments, people turn to people first. Networks are still the number one trusted source at work, according to a LinkedIn global survey. Not search engines. Not AI tools. Other people. So find your people. Share what you're learning and get inspired by what they're learning too.

EXERCISE:
- **Build your bench of experts to follow.** There are so many smart voices out there, from neuroscientists to researchers to AI product builders. Follow them on LinkedIn to stay on the cutting edge of how technology is reshaping your work. Staying on top of new advancements is going to be key, given how fast this technology is evolving. Follow five to ten experts you trust across different areas of expertise. A lot of the people in this book post helpful tips and advice if you're looking for a place to start.

- **Find peers to learn alongside.** While staying in the know with experts will help you feel more informed and confident in how you're testing and learning, it's actually your peers and people closer to you in your network who are more likely to open doors for you. Ask around and start to build your go-to group. Find people who are also on a similar journey whom you can connect and share learnings with. It could be people who work at your company who are exploring AI too. It could be someone you saw speak at a conference. It could be friends outside of work who you know are tech-savvy. Seek out three to five people and reach out to them to see if they're open to chatting and swapping ideas.
- **See what your company or manager can offer.** Raise the topic with your manager to see if your company is willing to support you in sharpening these new skills: Is there a course they're willing to pay for? An industry event they're open to sending you to? Another leader at the company willing to serve as your AI mentor in your upskilling efforts? Not every company will have the same resources and support available, but you will never know what's possible until you ask.
- **Share what you're learning.** Finally, one of the fastest ways to expand your network and find advocates you didn't know existed is to start sharing and teaching others about what you're learning. Commit to doing two to three things 'out loud' in these weeks: Comment your take on the next LinkedIn post you come across about AI in your industry, or share one thing you

learned this month with your network. That first bold act of admitting out loud you're working on this and are curious about it will hold you accountable to keep going.

Example: Ume completed five software engineering internships in three years. After countless technical interviews, she realized others could benefit from what she'd learned, especially young women in tech. Using AI to brainstorm content, she started posting tips on social media. She created analogies and visuals that resonated with people following her path. Now she has over twenty-six thousand LinkedIn followers, has connected with dozens of mentors and peers, and speaks at industry conferences. All because she decided to share what she was learning.

LinkedIn Pro Tip: Connection Fuels Opportunity

Think of conversations on LinkedIn not just as 'water cooler' talk: These are the conversations that spark your next big opportunity. People who comment on posts in their LinkedIn feed receive 2.5 times more profile views, and people who are more active and engaged in the LinkedIn feed see three times as many inbound connection requests. Your network is even likely sitting on AI know-how you need. Globally, we saw a 29 percent spike in 2025 in the number of people posting on LinkedIn about AI-related topics. The knowledge is out there. You just have to ask.

BY DAY 30, YOU'LL HAVE:
- Basic fluency with one to two AI tools to use on Bucket 2 tasks
- Clear vulnerability assessment
- Identified a handful of Bucket 1 tasks to start automating
- Connected with others on similar journeys

Days 31–60: Building Your 5Cs

By now, you should be getting the hang of using AI tools in your workday. But so far, these are likely just incremental wins. This next step is about setting yourself up for the big wins: wins that will carry you across your career. This month, the focus is on shoring up the most durable skills you'll need no matter how technology evolves. These are skills we often undervalue as 'soft' that are actually the most important survival skills in your career: the 5Cs.

Curiosity and Creativity – Generating New Ideas

Curiosity and creativity are two sides of the same coin. Curiosity is about asking better questions and exploring new possibilities. Creativity is about taking what you discover and turning it into something valuable. Together, they're a superpower for staying relevant. While AI can generate ideas, it can't wonder 'what if?' the way you can. It can't connect dots across seemingly unrelated experiences or bring fresh perspective shaped by your unique background. That's all you.

EXERCISE:
- **Find something that needs a refresh.** Identify one process, project, or challenge at work that feels stale or stuck. Maybe it's a weekly meeting that's lost its purpose, a client deliverable that's gone on autopilot for too long, or a team dynamic that needs fresh energy.
- **Spend a week in curiosity mode.** Research how others in different industries or roles have tackled similar challenges. Ask three people outside your immediate team how they'd approach it. Ask AI to surface unexpected parallels, such as by requesting examples from five industries you'd never normally look to. Cast a wider net than you normally would. The goal is to collect raw material and expand your thinking beyond your usual patterns.
- **Now shift into creativity mode.** Take everything you've learned and prototype one creative solution. This is where AI can be your brainstorming partner too. Use it to stress-test ideas, generate variations, or build a quick mock-up.

Example: Your team's quarterly planning meetings are predictable and uninspiring. You start asking around: How do other teams run their planning sessions? You discover a product team that uses a 'pre-mortem' exercise, in which they imagine the quarter failed and work backward from there. A sales team leader tells you they invite a customer to join part of their planning. A friend in consulting mentions their firm does 'innovation sprints' instead of traditional meetings. You take these insights and use AI to help you design a hybrid approach: a planning session that starts with a pre-mortem, includes a customer perspective video, and ends with breakout innovation sprints. You create a draft agenda and use AI to generate discussion prompts and timing suggestions. You pitch it to your manager. The next planning session becomes the most engaged your team has been in months.

Communication and Compassion – Building Human Connection

In a world where AI can draft the email, write the memo, and summarize the meeting, your ability to truly connect with other people becomes your most valuable currency. Great communication isn't simply the act of transmitting information clearly. It involves reading between the lines, adapting your message to your audience, and building the kind of trust that can't be automated. And compassion for whoever is on the other side of the table is what makes that message land. Compassion doesn't just happen; it's something we all need to work at by developing a genuine understanding of what someone else is experiencing, even when it's uncomfortable or inconvenient.

EXERCISE:
- **Pick one relationship at work that could use more investment.** Maybe it's a direct report who seems disengaged, a peer you've been butting heads with, or a stakeholder who never seems satisfied with your work. Commit to deepening that relationship over these two weeks.
- **Start by practicing active listening in your next conversation with them.** Put away your phone. Close your laptop. Ask open-ended questions and really hear what they're saying. Not just the words, but the emotion and context behind them. What pressures are they under? What do they care about that you might have missed? Use your curiosity to ask deeper questions to genuinely understand their world.
- **Pause to reflect on where they're coming from.** Before your next interaction, ask yourself, What does this person need from me right now to feel heard, supported, or effective? Is it clarity, reassurance, space, or problem-solving? Adjust your approach accordingly.
- **Then push yourself further: Have one difficult conversation you've been avoiding.** It could be giving feedback that's hard to hear, admitting you dropped the ball on something, or addressing a tension that's been simmering. Do it with compassion: Lead with understanding, be specific about impact, and focus on moving forward together.

Example: Neil has seen small acts of compassion alter team dynamics completely. He encourages members of the teams he coaches to call each other just to chat: 'Hey, how's it going? I'm going for a walk, do you want to join me? I'd love to hear how you're doing.' It's uncomfortable for most people, he says, but he's seen it fundamentally change a team's capacity to perform and make good decisions. The manager who notices an employee's performance dropping and discovers they're caring for a sick parent, then quietly arranges flexible hours. The customer service rep who stays on the phone longer than needed with a confused customer, walking her through each step.

Courage – Taking Bold Action

You've spent the past few weeks building capabilities and deepening relationships. Now it's time to take a leap of faith and do something that scares you a little. Courage doesn't mean you aren't afraid. It means acting despite the fear. AI will make many things easier, but it won't raise your hand for you. It won't take the risk of looking foolish. It won't push back when everyone else is nodding along. That takes courage, and it's entirely human.

EXERCISE:
- **Identify one bold action that requires you to be seen:** pitching an idea in a meeting with senior leaders, applying for a stretch role, or publishing your perspective

on industry changes. The key is that it can't be anonymous. You're attaching your name and reputation to it.

- **Before you take the leap, do your homework.** Tap AI for info and trusted peers for insight. Use AI to pressure-test your logic: Ask it to identify blind spots in your thinking or generate the strongest counter-arguments to your proposal. Then run your refined approach past a trusted peer who can speak from lived experience.
- **Then do the thing.** Raise your hand. Send the message. Have the conversation. Make the ask. You don't need permission to be courageous, but you do need to actually do it.
- **After you take your bold action, reflect on what happened.** Did it go as planned? Better? Worse? What did you learn? Most importantly, how does it feel to have done it? That feeling is what you're building toward: the confidence that comes from knowing you can bet on yourself.

Example: You're a junior in college. Summer internship season is fast-approaching and you're still empty-handed. You find a startup doing work you care about, but they're not hiring interns. You spend a weekend using AI to research their biggest challenges based on founder interviews. You find a mutual connection who gives you an inside scoop on the company culture and ways of working that AI can't capture. You create a short proposal for how an intern could help, complete with timeline and deliverables. You message the founder on LinkedIn. Three days later: 'We weren't planning to hire an intern, but this is exactly what we need. Can we talk?' That first conversation opens up an opportunity that didn't exist before.

> **LinkedIn Pro Tip: Showcase Your AI Skills and 5Cs on Your Profile**
>
> Your profile is a great place to show off not just all the new AI skills you're building, but your 5Cs too. Think of the About section as your elevator pitch, and your previous job descriptions as the training grounds where you built up critical skills and experiences. Be specific and think about how the story you're telling here will match up to the types of opportunities you're applying for out there. Read job descriptions and explore the profiles of people you admire for inspiration on things you might not think to showcase but should. Building this out goes a long way: LinkedIn members with at least one skill listed receive up to two times more profile views and connection requests, and four times as many messages. This is your opportunity to tell your story in your own words.

BY DAY 60, YOU'LL HAVE:
- Prototyped at least one creative solution to a real work challenge
- Strengthened a key relationship through intentional communication and compassion

- Taken one bold, visible action that expanded what you thought possible for yourself
- Started to build the muscle memory for exercising all 5Cs that will serve you for the rest of your career

Days 61–90: Transformation – Starting Your Climb

At this stage, you've hopefully built a strong foundation. You're fluent with AI tools, you've assessed your job vulnerability, and you've strengthened the human skills that will help you manage the change that's hitting work. Now it's time to put all the pieces together and chart your path forward as you think about your career.

As we discussed in chapter 6, there are three big questions to figure out on the career climbing wall: *Why* do you work, *what* do you uniquely do, and *where* are you going? You'll revisit and adjust your *why*, *what*, and *where* at every stage of your career. That means the answers you uncover today are not set in stone: they will evolve as your career evolves.

Question 1: *Why* Do You Work?

Every meaningful decision you make in your career should start with a fundamental question: *Why* do you do what you do in the first place? This question is about understanding what truly motivates you, even if it will change over time. As

OPEN TO WORK

Ethan reminds us, 'It is rare that what motivates someone at twenty will remain constant until fifty or sixty.' Having clarity about *why* you climb gives you the foundation to make every other decision with purpose.

EXERCISE:
- **Set aside thirty minutes of uninterrupted time.** Put away your phone and open a blank document. Write down your honest answers to these questions without editing yourself: When you imagine your career five years from now, what does success look like? Not what you think it should look like, but what *actually* excites you when you picture it. What are you doing? Who are you working with? What impact are you having? What does your day-to-day feel like?
- **Now go deeper:** Why does that version of success matter to you? What values or experiences are driving that vision? Keep asking why until you get to something that feels true and grounded in who you are, not who you think you should be.
- **Look back at your three buckets:** Which tasks in Buckets 2 and 3 energize you the most? Which problems do you find yourself thinking about even when you're not 'supposed' to be working? These are clues to your *why*.
- **Get an outside opinion.** Share your answers with two people who know you well, one at work, one outside of work. Ask them, Does this sound like me? What am I missing? Sometimes others can see our motivations more clearly than we can.

Example: Diego discovered his *why* early. Growing up in rural Texas, he watched his father lose his transportation business in 2008 and move three hours away to the oil fields for work. When Diego later dropped out of college and knew he wouldn't get hired for certain positions due to degree requirements, he chose what he calls the 'permissionless path.' Entrepreneurship became his North Star because it was the only avenue that didn't ask for permission. In 2017, he started a recruiting company. No credentials required. Just the grit to figure it out. And now he helps other rural entrepreneurs build businesses from home with the help of AI. Since then, his *why* has stayed clear: creating permissionless paths to opportunity because he's seen firsthand what happens when families have to choose between home and work.

Question 2: *What* Do You Uniquely Do?

Now that you know *why* you're climbing, you need to assess *what* you uniquely bring to the table that sets you apart. Your *what* is your particular mix of skills, experiences, curiosities, and capabilities. When AI can handle the generic, this specific combination keeps you on steady ground for the long run. Finding your *what* builds directly on the three buckets you created earlier on. You've already sorted your tasks into what AI can do, what you'll do with AI, and what only you can do. Now you need to look at those buckets, especially Buckets 2 and 3, and ask, What patterns do I see? Which capabilities show up again and again? Which problems do people always turn to me to solve?

EXERCISE:
- **List out all your unique skills.** Pull up your three buckets from the earlier exercise. Look specifically at Buckets 2 and 3: the work you do with AI and the uniquely human work. Write down every skill or capability those tasks require. Be specific. Don't just write 'communication'; write 'translating technical concepts for non-technical stakeholders' or 'defusing tense conversations between departments.'
- **Narrow down your top superpowers.** Once you have your list, identify your top three to five capabilities. These should be things you're genuinely good at *and* that you are excited to do *and* that are valued at work. Circle the ones that show up most frequently across your tasks.
- **Make sure your skills are visible.** Especially if you're on the job hunt, make sure these skills are also clearly listed on places like your LinkedIn profile: Do a quick skills audit on your profile, adding your unique skills under each past role and any certifications you may have earned along the way.
- **Now look for intersections.** Where do three or more of your capabilities overlap? This is where your *what* gets strong. As Ethan reminds us, 'You may not be the best at any one skill, but you may be among the very best at the combination of several of them.'

- **Identify one capability gap that's holding you back.** Use AI to close it enough to be competent, not expert. For example, if data visualization is your weakness, use AI tools to generate clean charts from your analysis, letting your pattern recognition and storytelling shine through.

Example: You're a customer success manager who's been doing the job for six years. You look at your three buckets and list your capabilities: active listening, pattern recognition across customer problems, translating pain into product requirements, staying calm under pressure, building trust quickly, data analysis, and storytelling. You notice several show up together constantly: You hear what frustrated customers are really saying, spot trends across dozens of complaints, translate that into compelling narratives for the product team, and back it up with data. That's your *what*. You're weak at data visualization. Your analysis is solid but your presentations are kind of boring. You experiment with AI tools that generate charts and dashboards from your analysis. Suddenly your presentations land differently. You're not becoming a data scientist. You're using AI to cover a weakness so your unique combination can shine through. Your *what*: 'I uniquely solve the problem of translating customer pain into product action because I combine deep empathy with pattern recognition across hundreds of conversations, and I craft narratives that make product teams care enough to act.'

OPEN TO WORK

Question 3: *Where* Are You Going?

Now you're ready to move. You've articulated the *why* that's driving your decisions. You've uncovered your *what* and you know the skills that make you strong. Your last step is translating that into forward motion: choosing *where* your path goes next. Figuring out your *where* is iterative. You'll adjust, pivot, and sometimes even backpedal as the job market or your situation changes and calls for a new direction. Agility is key here. As you reach one destination, whether it's the dream job you've long strived for or the business milestone you never thought your company would cross, you might get there and uncover a new *why* that calls for you to start over and try a different path next.

EXERCISE:
- **Explore where your *why* meets your *what*.** Pull up your *why* and your *what* from the earlier exercises. Write them out and look at them side by side. Now ask, *Where* in the world of work do these two things intersect? What roles, projects, or opportunities would let me use my unique skills to climb toward my ultimate goal?
- **Make a list of three to five possible paths.** These don't have to be specific job titles; they can be descriptions of work. Think broadly. Consider roles that might be adjacent to what you do now. Consider entrepreneurial paths. Consider lateral moves that seem 'off track' but align with your *why*.

- **Learn from people who have already gone down those paths.** Before jumping into hitting apply, do a quick search for other people in your network with similar job titles to the type of work that interests you. Reach out and send a message to two to three of them to see if they are up for a chat so you can learn more about what those jobs are really like day-to-day.
- **Evaluate your potential paths.** Once you have a better sense of which path feels right for you, evaluate it against three criteria: Does it leverage my *what*? (Will I get to use my unique combination of capabilities?) Does it move me toward my *why*? (Does it align with my North Star?) Is it realistic in the next six to twelve months? (Do I have the foundational capabilities, or can I go build them?)
- **Then, start with the *where* that scores highest across all three.** This is likely your primary path. It could be a job title, it could be a company, it could be a new business idea. Pick one backup path that also scores well. This is your plan B.
- **Now make it concrete.** What are the next three moves you need to make to start climbing this path? These should be specific actions, not vague intentions. 'Network with people in X field' is vague. 'Reach out to five people doing Y role and ask for twenty-minute informational conversations' is specific. Commit to taking that first step within the next week.

OPEN TO WORK

Example: John Henry grew up in New York, the son of Dominican immigrants, his mother a janitor and his father a presser at a dry cleaner. Working as a doorman to put himself through community college, he dreamed of leaving his working-class roots behind until getting fired forced a reckoning. His *why*: earning a living and achieving financial security. His *what*: deep industry knowledge learned from his father and an instinct for spotting overlooked opportunities. His *where*: building businesses where those 'disadvantages' became advantages. That began with a wash-and-fold side hustle that landed *The Wolf of Wall Street*'s costume account and grew into a million-dollar company by the time he was twenty-one. From there, he built an incubator in Harlem, founded a car insurance startup fighting bias, and joined an investment firm, each move grounded in turning lived experience into leverage and helping others do the same.

> **LinkedIn Pro Tip: Discover Potential Routes**
>
> Stuck on which routes are even out there? Use LinkedIn's AI-powered job search to explore roles that match your *why* and *what*. Head to the Jobs tab and describe your ideal work in plain language: 'I want a role in finance that helps the environment' or 'I want to work in marketing for entertainment companies.' Set up Job Seeking Preferences to filter for more granular factors like whether you want remote, hybrid, or contract work. This makes it easier for the right opportunities to find you. Once you identify promising routes, turn on job alerts. The job market moves fast, so mapping out your route now and being ready when opportunity strikes is key.

BY DAY 90, YOU'LL HAVE:
- Defined your *why*: your unique reason for climbing
- Identified your *what*: the combination of capabilities that only you bring
- Charted your *where*: a concrete path forward based on what makes you uniquely you

You'll finish these ninety days not just more AI-fluent or more skilled, but more confident in your ability to adapt, and more ready to help others do the same. You won't just be navigating the future of work. You'll be writing your story into it.

Acknowledgments

To every past, present, and future employee at LinkedIn and Microsoft, we end with gratitude. We show up to work every day to create economic opportunity for the global workforce and to empower every person and organization in the world to achieve more. That is always true, but it is especially true in moments of big change, when we all feel an extra responsibility to help professionals connect, learn, work, and grow in new ways, together.

Notes

Foreword

1. World Bank Group, Independent Evaluation Group, *An Evaluation of the World Bank Group's Support to Electricity Access in Sub-Saharan Africa, 2015–24: Approach Paper* (Washington, DC: World Bank Group, Feb. 19, 2025), https://ieg.worldbankgroup.org/sites/default/files/Data/reports/Ap_WBG_Elec_Africa_2015-24.pdf.

Introduction: Failure Is Not an Option

1. Richard Goldstein, 'James A. Lovell Jr., Commander of Apollo 13, Is Dead at 97,' *New York Times*, Aug. 8, 2025, www.nytimes.com/2025/08/08/science/space/james-a-lovell-jr-dead.html.
2. Heather Deiss, 'The Hard-Won Triumph of the Apollo 13 Mission – 45 Years Later,' NASA, May 3, 2023, www.nasa.gov/missions/apollo/the-hard-won-triumph-of-the-apollo-13-mission-45-years-later/.

3. Joseph B. Treaster, 'Jack Swigert, Astronaut Elected to Congress, Dies,' *New York Times*, Dec. 29, 1982, https://www.nytimes.com/1982/12/29/obituaries/jack-swigert-astronaut-elected-to-congress-dies.html.
4. 'Apollo 13: Mission Details,' NASA, July 8, 2009, www.nasa.gov/missions/apollo/apollo-13-mission-details.
5. Jim Lovell and Jeffrey Kluger, *Lost Moon: The Perilous Voyage of Apollo 13* (Boston: Houghton Mifflin, 1994), 95–97.
6. 'Apollo 13 Flight Journal – Day 3, Part 2: "Houston, We've Had a Problem,"' NASA, Aug. 1, 2025, https://www.nasa.gov/history/alsj-and-afj/.
7. 'Apollo 13,' The Planetary Society, accessed Dec. 14, 2025, https://www.planetary.org/space-missions/apollo-13.
8. 'Lithium Hydroxide Canister, Mock-up, Apollo 13 Emergency,' Smithsonian National Air and Space Museum, NASM A19760747000, accessed Dec. 14, 2025, https://airandspace.si.edu/collection-objects/lithium-hydroxide-canister-mock-apollo-13-emergency/nasm_A19760747000.
9. John L. Goodman, 'Apollo 13 Guidance, Navigation, and Control Challenges,' NASA Technical Reports Server, Sept. 17, 2009, https://ntrs.nasa.gov/api/citations/20090026451/downloads/20090026451.pdf.
10. Richard D. Lyons, '12 Countries Offer to Help In Recovery of Astronauts,' *New York Times*, April 16, 1970, https://www.nytimes.com/1970/04/16/archives/12-countries-offer-to-help-in-recovery-of-astronauts-12-countries.html.
11. Kyle Wiggers, Cody Corrall, and Alyssa Stringer, 'ChatGPT: Everything Released from the AI-Powered Chatbot in 2022,'

Notes

TechCrunch, Dec. 31, 2022, techcrunch.com/2022/12/31/chatgpt-everything-released-from-the-ai-powered-chatbot-in-2022/#nov22.

12. Charles Duhigg, 'The Inside Story of Microsoft's Partnership with OpenAI,' *New Yorker*, Dec. 1, 2023, www.newyorker.com/magazine/2023/12/11/the-inside-story-of-microsofts-partnership-with-openai.
13. Goldstein, 'James A. Lovell Jr., Commander of Apollo 13, Is Dead at 97.'

Chapter 1: Buckle Up

1. 'Work Change Report: AI Is Coming to Work,' LinkedIn, Jan. 2025, economicgraph.linkedin.com/content/dam/me/economicgraph/en-us/PDF/Work-Change-Report.pdf.
2. 'Now Comes the Hard Part,' 2024 Work Trend Index Annual Report, May 8, 2024, https://blogs.microsoft.com/blog/2024/05/08/microsoft-and-linkedin-release-the-2024-work-trend-index-on-the-state-of-ai-at-work/.
3. Microsoft and LinkedIn, 'AI at Work Is Here.'
4. 'LinkedIn Skills on the Rise 2025: The 15 Fastest-Growing in the U.S.,' LinkedIn News, March 19, 2025, https://www.linkedin.com/pulse/linkedin-skills-rise-2025-15-fastest-growing-us-linkedin-news-hy0le/.
5. 'Future of Skills,' LinkedIn, accessed Nov. 23, 2025, https://linkedin.github.io/future-of-skills/.
6. Robert Smith, host, *Planet Money*, podcast, 'Summer School 5: Tech and the Innovator's Dilemma,' NPR, Aug. 9, 2023, https://www.npr.org/transcripts/1192918768.

7. Alexander Lee, 'The War Against Printing,' Engelsberg Ideas, Aug. 1, 2022, https://engelsbergideas.com/essays/the-war-against-printing/.
8. Stephen Heyman, 'Photos, Photos Everywhere,' *New York Times*, July 29, 2015, https://www.nytimes.com/2015/07/23/arts/international/photos-photos-everywhere.html.
9. Lewis Carroll, *Through the Looking-Glass, and What Alice Found There*, Project Gutenberg Ebook 12, Millennium Fulcrum Edition 1.7, www.gutenberg.org/files/12/12-h/12-h.htm.
10. LinkedIn, 'Work Change Report: AI Is Coming to Work.'
11. Habiba, interview for book, July 15, 2025.
12. 'Why did the Luddites protest?' The National Archives, accessed Nov. 18, 2025, https://www.nationalarchives.gov.uk/education/resources/why-did-the-luddites-protest/.
13. Peter Dizikes, 'Most Work Is New Work, Long-Term Study of U.S. Census Data Shows,' *MIT News*, April 1, 2024, https://news.mit.edu/2024/most-work-is-new-work-us-census-data-shows-0401.
14. Philip Soundy Unwin, George Unwin, and David H. Tucker, 'The Age of Early Printing: 1450–1550,' in 'History of Publishing,' *Encyclopedia Britannica*, Sept. 8, 2025, accessed Nov. 18, 2025, https://www.britannica.com/topic/publishing/The-age-of-early-printing-1450-1550.
15. Jonetta Gresham, interview for book, July 24, 2025.

Notes

Chapter 2: Let It Go

1. Sitalla Peek, 'Knocker Uppers: Waking Up the Workers in Industrial Britain,' *BBC News*, March 27, 2016, www.bbc.com/news/uk-england-35840393.
2. Paula Mejia, 'Remembering the "Knocker-Ups" Hired to Wake Workers with Pea Shooters,' *Atlas Obscura*, May 18, 2018, www.atlasobscura.com/articles/what-did-people-use-before-alarm-clocks.
3. 'Shoes + Shoemaking,' Maine MILL, accessed Oct. 22, 2025, https://mainemill.org/learn/for-teachers/shoes-shoemaking/.
4. Hillary Taylor, 'Fatal Labour Discipline in Early Modern England,' Forms of Labour, University of Exeter, accessed Dec. 12, 2025, https://formsoflabour.exeter.ac.uk/conference/fatal-labour-discipline-in-early-modern-england/.
5. Judy Stephenson, 'Industriousness and Precarity: Work before the Industrial Revolution,' *Top of the Campops*, Cambridge Group for the History of Population and Social Structure, University of Cambridge, May 15, 2025, https://www.campop.geog.cam.ac.uk/blog/2025/05/15/precarity-in-work/.
6. National Child Labor Committee Collection, Prints and Photographs Division, Library of Congress, Washington, D.C., accessed Dec. 12, 2025, https://www.loc.gov/collections/national-child-labor-committee/.
7. 'Health, Safety and Welfare at Work,' Science Museum, Jan. 10, 2024, https://www.sciencemuseum.org.uk/objects-and-stories/health-safety-and-welfare-work.
8. Judson MacLaury, 'A Brief History: The U.S. Department of Labor,' in *A Historical Guide to the U.S. Government*, ed. George T. Kurian (Oxford: Oxford University Press, 1998),

9. Max Roser, 'The Short History of Global Living Conditions and Why It Matters That We Know It,' Our World in Data, last revised Feb. 2024, https://ourworldindata.org/a-history-of-global-living-conditions.
10. Saloni Dattani et al., 'Life Expectancy,' Our World in Data, accessed Dec. 12, 2025, https://ourworldindata.org/life-expectancy.
11. Esteban Ortiz-Ospina, 'Two Centuries Ago, Only 1 in 10 Adults Could Read. Today, It's Almost 9 in 10,' Our World in Data, July 29, 2024, https://ourworldindata.org/data-insights/two-centuries-ago-only-1-in-10-adults-could-read-today-its-almost-9-in-10.
12. Max Roser, Saloni Dattani, Fiona Spooner, and Hannah Ritchie, 'Child and Infant Mortality,' Our World in Data, last modified in 2023, data adapted from United Nations Inter-agency Group for Child Mortality Estimation, Gapminder based on UN IGME & UN WPP, and various sources, accessed Dec. 12, 2025, https://ourworldindata.org/grapher/child-mortality-complete-gapminder?time=earliest.
13. United Nations, 'Goal 1: End Poverty in All Its Forms Everywhere,' section of *The Sustainable Development Goals Report 2025* (New York: United Nations, 2025), https://unstats.un.org/sdgs/report/2025/goal-01/.
14. Katharina Bucholz, 'This is How Much the Global Literacy Rate Grew Over 200 Years,' World Economic Forum, Sept. 12, 2022, https://www.weforum.org/stories/2022/09/reading-writing-global-literacy-rate-changed/.

(Note: item 8 continues at top) revised, https://www.dol.gov/general/aboutdol/history/dolhistoxford.

Notes

15. Saloni Dattani et al., 'Life Expectancy.'
16. 'Ford Gives $10,000,000 To 26,000 Employees,' *New York Times*, Jan. 5, 1914, https://web.archive.org/web/20120115214241/https://www.nytimes.com/learning/general/onthisday/big/0105.html#article; Ellen Terrell, '40 Hours, 5 Days,' Inside Adams: Science, Technology & Business, *Library of Congress Blogs*, Jan. 17, 2024, https://blogs.loc.gov/inside_adams/2024/01/40-hours-5-days/.
17. Michael Dalton and Jeffrey A. Groen, 'Telework During the COVID-19 Pandemic: Estimates Using the 2021 Business Response Survey,' *Monthly Labor Review*, U.S. Bureau of Labor Statistics, March 2022, doi.org/10.21916/mlr.2022.8.
18. Louise Kapp Howe, *Pink Collar Workers: Inside the World of Women's Work* (G. P. Putnam and Sons, 1977).
19. 'History,' Harvard Business School, accessed Oct. 22, 2025, https://www.hbs.edu/about/history.
20. LinkedIn, 'Work Change Report: AI Is Coming to Work.'
21. Natasha Singer, 'Goodbye, $165,000 Tech Jobs. Student Coders Seek Work at Chipotle,' *New York Times*, Aug. 10, 2025, www.nytimes.com/2025/08/10/technology/coding-ai-jobs-students.html.
22. 'The Labor Market for Recent College Graduates,' Federal Reserve Bank of New York, Feb. 20, 2025, www.newyorkfed.org/research/college-labor-market#--:explore:outcomes-by-major.
23. Taylor Borden, 'LinkedIn Guide to Future-Proofing Your Career: What to Know About Evolving Jobs, In-Demand Skills and Strategic Moves in the Age of AI,' LinkedIn News, Sept. 29, 2025, https://www.linkedin.com/pulse/linkedin-

guide-future-proofing-your-career-what-know-evolving-giyqc/.
24. 'Breaking Down the Infinite Workday,' WorkLab, Microsoft Word Trend Index Special Report, June 17, 2025, https://www.microsoft.com/en-us/worklab/work-trend-index/breaking-down-infinite-workday.
25. Anne-Marie Slaughter, interview for book, Aug. 1, 2025.
26. Zachary Green and Gili Malinsky, 'Gen Z Workers Increasingly Opt Out of College and Into the Trades: "There Are About 2 Million Fewer Students," Says Expert,' CNBC, April 24, 2025, https://www.cnbc.com/2025/04/24/gen-z-workers-opt-out-of-college-and-go-into-trades.html.
27. Paul Cheek, interview for book, Sept. 23, 2025.
28. 'Academics,' MIT Schwarzman College of Computing, accessed Nov. 24, 2025, https://computing.mit.edu/academics/.
29. Neil Pretty, interview for book, July 22, 2025.
30. Nataliya Kosmyna et al., 'Your Brain on ChatGPT: Accumulation of Cognitive Debt When Using an AI Assistant for Essay Writing Task' (Preprint, submitted in 2025), arXiv:2506.08872, https://arxiv.org/abs/2506.08872.
31. Cheek, interview for book, Sept. 23, 2025.
32. Taj English, interview for book, July 24, 2025.
33. Microsoft and LinkedIn, 'AI at Work Is Here.'

Chapter 3: The Humans Are Coming
1. Ladislav Kováč, 'The 20 W Sleep-Walkers,' *EMBO Reports* 11, no. 1 (2010): 2, doi.org/10.1038/embor.2009.266.

Notes

2. P. Hartmann et al., 'Normal Weight of the Brain in Adults in Relation to Age, Sex, Body Height, and Weight' [in German], *Der Pathologe* 15 (1994): 165–70, doi.org/10.1007/s002920050040.
3. Michael S. Rosenwald, 'Eleanor Maguire, Memory Expert Who Studied London Cabbies, Dies at 54,' *New York Times*, Feb. 14, 2025, www.nytimes.com/2025/02/14/science/eleanor-maguire-dead.html.
4. E. A. Maguire et al., 'Navigation-Related Structural Change in the Hippocampi of Taxi Drivers,' *Proceedings of the National Academy of Sciences* 97, no. 8 (2000): 4398–403, doi.org/10.1073/pnas.070039597.
5. K. Anders Ericsson, Michael J. Prietula, and Edward T. Cokely, 'The Making of an Expert,' *Harvard Business Review*, July/Aug. 2007, https://hbr.org/2007/07/the-making-of-an-expert.
6. Anders Ericsson and Robert Pool, *Peak: Secrets from the New Science of Expertise* (New York: HarperCollins, 2016), Kindle edition.
7. A. Sakakibara, 'A Longitudinal Study of the Process of Acquiring Absolute Pitch: A Practical Report of Training with the "Chord Identification Method,"' *Psychology of Music* 42, no. 1 (2012): 86–111, https://doi.org/10.1177/0305735612463948.
8. Ericsson and Pool, *Peak*, Kindle edition.
9. Marc Brysbaert and Serge Nicolas, 'Two Persistent Myths About Binet and the Beginnings of Intelligence Tests in Psychology Textbooks,' *Collabra: Psychology* 10, no. 1 (2024): 117600, doi.org/10.1525/collabra.117600.

10. Joel Michell, 'Alfred Binet and the Concept of Heterogeneous Orders,' *Frontiers in Psychology* 3, (2012): 261, doi.org/10.3389/fpsyg.2012.00261.
11. Kylie Tuppin, Ben W. Morrison, and Joanne Kaa Earl, 'Psychological Assessment for Military Selection: Past, Present and Future Applications,' *Journal of Military and Veterans' Health* 33, no. 4 (2025), https://jmvh.org/article/psychological-assessment-for-military-selection-past-present-and-future-applications/.
12. Katherine Bindley, Corrie Driebusch, and Lindsay Ellis, 'Computer-Science Majors Graduate into a World of Fewer Opportunities,' *Wall Street Journal*, May 20, 2024, www.wsj.com/lifestyle/careers/computer-science-majors-job-market-7ad443bf?st.
13. Aneesh Raman and Maria Flynn, 'When Your Technical Skills Are Eclipsed, Your Humanity Will Matter More Than Ever,' *New York Times*, Feb. 14, 2024, https://www.nytimes.com/2024/02/14/opinion/ai-economy-jobs-colleges.html.
14. Ming, interview for book, July 30, 2025.
15. Vivienne Ming, 'Making a Better Person | Vivienne Ming | TEDxBerkeley,' posted May 5, 2017, by TEDx Talks, YouTube, https://www.youtube.com/watch?v=5-aIq4cRlss.
16. Ming, interview for book, July 30, 2025.
17. 'About Jonas Salk,' Salk Institute for Biological Studies, accessed Aug. 1, 2025, www.salk.edu/about/history-of-salk/jonas-salk/.
18. Gresham, interview for book.
19. Habiba, interview for book.

Notes

20. Ed Yong, 'Deformed Skull of Prehistoric Child Suggests That Early Humans Cared for Disabled Children,' *National Geographic*, March 30, 2009, https://www.nationalgeographic.com/science/article/deformed-skull-of-prehistoric-child-suggests-that-early-humans-cared-for-disabled-children.

21. Kim Armstrong, '"I Feel Your Pain": The Neuroscience of Empathy,' Association for Psychological Science, Dec. 29, 2017, https://www.psychologicalscience.org/observer/neuroscience-empathy.

22. Pretty, interview for book.

23. Dan Brodnitz, 'The Most In-Demand Skills for 2024,' LinkedIn Talent Blog, Feb. 8, 2024, www.linkedin.com/business/talent/blog/talent-strategy/linkedin-most-in-demand-hard-and-soft-skills.

24. Cheek, interview for book.

25. 'Daniel Goleman,' accessed Nov. 24, 2025. https://www.danielgoleman.info/. For more important research on emotional intelligence, see Peter Salovey and John D. Mayer, 'Emotional Intelligence,' *Imagination, Cognition and Personality* 9, no. 3 (1990): 185–211, https://doi.org/10.2190/DUGG-P24E-52WK-6CDG.

26. Walter Isaacson, *Leonardo da Vinci* (New York: Simon & Schuster, 2017), 685, Kindle edition.

27. Isaacson, *Leonardo da Vinci*, 685, Kindle edition.

28. Isaacson, *Leonardo da Vinci*, 690, Kindle edition.

29. Isaacson, *Leonardo da Vinci*, 685, Kindle edition.

Chapter 4: The Lost Einsteins

1. Alex Bell et al., 'Who Becomes an Inventor in America? The Importance of Exposure to Innovation,' Equality of Opportunity, Nov. 2018, www.equality-of-opportunity.org/assets/documents/inventors_paper.pdf.
2. Gareth Cook, 'The Economist Who Would Fix the American Dream,' *The Atlantic*, Aug. 2019, https://www.theatlantic.com/magazine/archive/2019/08/raj-chettys-american-dream/592804/.
3. Bell et al., 'Who Becomes an Inventor in America?', 1.
4. Bell et al., 'Who Becomes an Inventor in America?' 3.
5. Joaquín Rodríguez-Vidal et al., 'A Rock Engraving Made by Neanderthals in Gibraltar,' *Proceedings of the National Academy of Sciences* 111, no. 37 (2014): 13301–6, doi.org/10.1073/pnas.1411529111.
6. Michael Tomasello, Anne Cale Kruger, and Hilary Horn Ratner, 'Cultural Learning,' *Behavorial and Brain Sciences* 16, no. 3 (1993): 495–511, https://doi.org/10.1017/S0140525X003123X.
7. Eiluned Pearce, 'Neanderthals and Homo sapiens: Cognitively Different Kinds of Human?,' in *Evolution of Primate Social Cognition*, ed. Laura Desirèe Di Paolo, Fabio Di Vincenzo, and Francesca De Petrillo (Cham: Springer, 2018), 181–196.
8. Pringle, 'The Origin of Human Creativity Was Surprisingly Complex.'
9. F. Richard Stephenson, 'Chinese and Korean Star Maps and Catalogs,' in *History of Cartography*, Vol. 2, Book 2, ed. J. B. Harley and David Woodward (Chicago: University of

Notes

Chicago Press, 1994), https://press.uchicago.edu/books/hoc/HOC_V2_B2/HOC_VOLUME2_Book2_chapter13.pdf.

10. Marika Sardar, 'Astronomy and Astrology in the Medieval Islamic World,' Met, Aug. 1, 2011, www.metmuseum.org/essays/astronomy-and-astrology-in-the-medieval-islamic-world.

11. George Saliba, 'Arabic/Islamic Science and the Renaissance Science in Italy,' Columbia University (web project), 1999, accessed Dec. 12, 2025, https://www.columbia.edu/~gas1/project/visions/case1/sci.2.html.

12. F. Jamil Ragep, 'Copernicus and His Islamic Predecessors: Some Historical Remarks,' *History of Science* 45 (2007): 65–81, https://adsabs.harvard.edu/full/2007HisSc..45...65R.

13. David Boyd Haycock, 'Chapter 1: "Standing on the Sholders of Giants,"' in *William Stukeley: Science, Religion and Archaeology in Eighteenth-Century England* (2002), published online Oct. 2005, The Newton Project, accessed Nov. 19, 2025, https://www.newtonproject.ox.ac.uk/view/texts/diplomatic/OTHE00018.

14. Bell et al., 'Who Becomes an Inventor in America?', 33.

15. Ruchir Agarwal and Patrick Gaule, 'Invisible Geniuses: Could the Knowledge Frontier Advance Faster?' *American Economic Review: Insights* 2, no. 4 (2020): 409–24, https://www.aeaweb.org/articles?id=10.1257/aeri.20190457.

16. Philippe Aghion et al., 'Living the American Dream in Finland: The Social Mobility of Inventors,' working paper, July 18, 2016, https://conference.nber.org/confer/2016/SI2016/PRINN/Aghion_Akcigit_Hyytinen_Toivanen.pdf.

17. Rebecca Linke, 'Lost Einsteins: The US May Have Missed Out on Millions of Inventors,' MIT Management, Feb. 16, 2018, mitsloan.mit.edu/ideas-made-to-matter/lost-einsteins-us-may-have-missed-out-millions-inventors.
18. Ming, interview for book, July 30, 2025.
19. Tess Posner, interview for book, Aug. 7, 2025.
20. Joséphine Goube, interview for book, Aug. 19, 2025.
21. Diego Arambula, interview for book, Aug. 8, 2025.
22. 'AP Career Kickstart,' AP Central, College Board, accessed Nov. 24, 2025, https://apcentral.collegeboard.org/courses/ap-career-kickstart.
23. Cheek, interview for book, Sept. 23, 2025.
24. 'Computer Science and Philosophy,' University of Illinois Urbana-Champaign, accessed Nov. 19, 2025, https://myillini.illinois.edu/Programs/MajorDetail/10KV5679BSLA.
25. 'About the Department of Digital Humanities,' Department of Digital Humanities, King's College London, accessed Nov. 11, 2025, https://www.kcl.ac.uk/ddh/about/about.
26. 'Applied Humanities Recognized for Innovation in New Report,' College of Humanities, University of Arizona, Nov. 8, 2024. https://humanities.arizona.edu/news/applied-humanities-recognized-innovation-new-report.
27. 'Applied Humanities Bachelor's Degree Online,' Oregon State University Ecampus, accessed Nov. 19, 2025, https://ecampus.oregonstate.edu/online-degrees/undergraduate/applied-humanities/.
28. Auzinea Bacon, 'Nvidia's Jensen Huang Says AI Could Lead to Job Losses "If the World Runs Out of Ideas,"' CNN,

Notes

July 11, 2025, www.cnn.com/2025/07/11/business/nvidia-jensen-huang-ai-job-loss.

Chapter 5: Jobs Are Tasks, Not Titles

1. 'Bette Graham: Liquid Paper,' Lemelson, MIT, Aug. 1, 2025, lemelson.mit.edu/resources/bette-graham.
2. Andrew R. Chow, 'Overlooked No More: Bette Nesmith Graham, Who Invented Liquid Paper,' *New York Times*, July 11, 2018, https://www.nytimes.com/2018/07/11/obituaries/bette-nesmith-graham-overlooked.html.
3. Adam Grant, Justin Berg, and Daniel Cable, 'Job Titles as Identity Badges: How Self-Reflective Titles Can Reduce Emotional Exhaustion,' *Academy of Management Journal* 57, no. 4 (2014): 1201–25, wpa.wharton.upenn.edu/content/academic-papers/self-reflective-titles/.
4. Louise Lee, 'Should Employees Design Their Own Jobs?' Insights by Stanford Business, Jan. 22, 2016, https://www.gsb.stanford.edu/insights/should-employees-design-their-own-jobs; Justin M. Berg, Jane E. Dutton, and Amy Wrzesniewski, 'What Is Job Crafting and Why Does It Matter?' Center for Positive Organizational Scholarship, University of Michigan, revised Aug. 1, 2008, https://positiveorgs.bus.umich.edu/wp-content/uploads/What-is-Job-Crafting-and-Why-Does-it-Matter1.pdf.
5. Microsoft and LinkedIn, 'AI at Work Is Here.'
6. Ming, interview for book.
7. Cheek, interview for book.

8. 'The Future of Jobs Report 2025,' World Economic Forum, Jan. 7, 2025, www.weforum.org/publications/the-future-of-jobs-report-2025/.
9. Curt R. Miller, 'Machines – The New Bank Tellers,' *New York Times*, Dec. 2, 1973, https://www.nytimes.com/1973/12/02/archives/machines-the-new-bank-tellers-response-to-automated-transactions-is.html.
10. Tess Townsend, 'Eric Schmidt Said ATMs Led to More Jobs for Bank Tellers. It's not that simple,' *Vox*, May 8, 2017, https://www.vox.com/2017/5/8/15584268/eric-schmidt-alphabet-automation-atm-bank-teller.
11. James Bessen, 'Toil and Technology,' *Finance & Development* 52, no. 1 (2015): 16–19, https://www.imf.org/external/pubs/ft/fandd/2015/03/bessen.htm.
12. David Autor, 'Will Automation Take Away All Our Jobs?', Ideas.TED.com, March 29, 2017, https://ideas.ted.com/will-automation-take-away-all-our-jobs/.
13. Katherine Townsend Kiernan, 'The Case of the Vanishing Teller: How Banking's Entry Level Jobs Are Transforming,' Burning Glass Institute, May 12, 2025, https://www.burningglassinstitute.org/bginsights/the-case-of-the-vanishing-teller-how-bankings-entry-level-jobs-are-transforming; Michael Rieley, 'In the Money: Occupational Projections for the Financial Industry,' *Beyond the Numbers: Employment & Unemployment* 7, no. 16. (U.S. Bureau of Labor Statistics, Oct. 26, 2018), https://www.bls.gov/opub/btn/volume-7/in-the-money-occupational-projections-for-the-financial-industry.htm; Rajesh Narayanan, Dimuthu Ratnadiwakara, and Philip E. Strahan, 'The Decline of

Notes

Branch Banking,' SSRN Scholarly Paper, Sept. 2025, https://doi.org/10.2139/ssrn.5105791.

Chapter 6: Careers Are Climbing Walls, Not Ladders
1. Adam Killick, 'This Woman Who Scaled a 2,600-Metre Mountain Face Says She "Proudly Checks the Disability Box,"' CBC, April 15, 2023, www.cbc.ca/radio/sunday/mountaineer-maureen-beck-1.6811280.
2. 'Maureen "Mo" Beck – Standing Alone: Being the First of YOU,' posted May 14, 2024, by Memphis Rox Climbing + Community, YouTube, 2025, https://www.youtube.com/watch?v=T49-NudoYbs.
3. Erik Weihenmayer, host, *No Barriers*, podcast, episode 90, 'Pushing Limits with Maureen Beck,' Jan. 6, 2021, nobarriersusa.org/podcast/interview-with-maureen-beck/.
4. Audrey Cleo Yap, 'How One-Handed Rock Climber Maureen Beck Became a Four-Time National Champion in Her Sport,' ESPN.com, Nov. 9, 2017, www.espn.com/espnw/life-style/story/_/id/21355139/how-one-handed-rock-climber-maureen-beck-became-four-national-champion-sport.
5. William H. Whyte, *The Organization Man* (New York: Simon & Schuster, 1956).
6. 'Work Change Report: AI Is Coming to Work.'
7. Douglas T. Hall, 'The Protean Career: A Quarter-Century Journey,' *Journal of Vocational Behavior* 65, no. 1 (2004): 1–13, doi.org/10.1016/j.jvb.2003.10.006.
8. Glenn Rifkin, 'Charles Handy Dies at 92; Philosopher Envisioned Today's Corporate World,' *New York Times*,

Dec. 13, 2024, www.nytimes.com/2024/12/13/business/charles-handy-dead.html.
9. Michael B. Arthur and Denise M. Rousseau, eds. *The Boundaryless Career: A New Employment Principle for a New Organizational Era* (Oxford: Oxford University Press, 1996).
10. Herminia Ibarra, *Working Identity: Unconventional Strategies for Reinventing Your Career*, 2nd ed. (Boston: Harvard Business Review Press, 2023).
11. 'About,' Amazing If, accessed Aug. 1, 2025, www.amazingif.com/about/.
12. Ethan Evans, interview for book, July 30, 2025.
13. Gresham, interview for book, July 24, 2025.
14. Cheek, interview for book, Sept. 23, 2025.
15. Diego A. Rubio, interview for book, July 24, 2025.
16. 'LinkedIn's Economic Graph: A Digital Representation of the Global Economy,' LinkedIn, accessed Nov. 23, 2025, https://economicgraph.linkedin.com/.

Chapter 7: Companies Are Work Charts, Not Org Charts

1. Warren D. Devine, 'From Shafts to Wires: Historical Perspective on Electrification,' *The Journal of Economic History* 43, no. 2 (1983): 347–72, https://doi.org/10.1017/S0022050700029673.
2. Jon Bruner, 'The Latest Technology Isn't Enough – You Need the Business Model to Go with It,' World Economic Forum, April 5, 2019, www.weforum.org/stories/2019/04/the-latest-technology-isnt-enough-you-need-the-business-model-to-go-with-it/.

Notes

3. 'Fine Printing Done by Electric Power,' *Electrical World*, 15 (1890), 432, https://babel.hathitrust.org/cgi/pt?id=mdp.39015048964269&seq=472.
4. 'Fine Printing Done by Electric Power.'
5. Tim Harford, 'What the History of the Electric Dynamo Teaches About the Future of the Computer,' *Slate*, June 9, 2007, https://slate.com/culture/2007/06/what-the-history-of-the-electric-dynamo-teaches-about-the-future-of-the-computer.html.
6. 'Belt & Lineshaft System – the transfer power in a 19th century machine shop,' posted April 12, 2018, by Charles River Museum of Industry & Innovation, YouTube, https://www.youtube.com/watch?v=7qt5tltnvF8.
7. Harford, 'What the History of the Electric Dynamo Teaches.'
8. Paul A. David, 'The Dynamo and the Computer: An Historical Perspective on the Modern Productivity Paradox,' *American Economic Review* 80, no. 2 (1990): 355–61, www.jstor.org/stable/2006600.
9. '2025: The Year the Frontier Firm Is Born,' Microsoft Work Trend Index Annual Report, April 23, 2025, https://www.microsoft.com/en-us/worklab/work-trend-index/2025-the-year-the-frontier-firm-is-born.
10. LinkedIn Talent Solutions, 'Conversations with CHROs: Aneesh Raman of LinkedIn with Eric Dozier from Eli Lilly and Company,' YouTube, March 17, 2025, https://www.youtube.com/watch?v=6EENo-q8P9U.
11. Grennan, interview for book, Sept. 24, 2025.
12. Liz Stinson, 'The First Org Chart Ever Made Is a Masterpiece of Data Design,' *WIRED*, March 18, 2014,

www.wired.com/2014/03/stunningly-complex-organization-chart-19th-century/.
13. '2025: The Year the Frontier Firm Is Born.'
14. Ming, interview for book.
15. Clayton M. Christensen, *The Innovator's Dilemma: When New Technologies Cause Great Firms to Fail* (Boston: Harvard Business Review Press, 2016).
16. Microsoft Corporate Blogs, 'Introducing CoreAI – Platform and Tools,' *Official Microsoft Blog*, Jan. 13, 2025, blogs.microsoft.com/blog/2025/01/13/introducing-core-ai-platform-and-tools/.
17. Sarah Nassauer and Chip Cutter, 'Walmart CEO Issues Wake-Up Call: "AI Is Going to Change Literally Every Job,"' Technology, *Wall Street Journal*, Sept. 26, 2025, https://www.wsj.com/tech/ai/walmart-ceo-doug-mcmillon-ai-job-losses-dbaca3aa?.
18. Jane Fraser, 'Remarks by CEO Jane Fraser at Citi's 2025 Annual Stockholders' Meeting,' Citigroup.com, April 29, 2025, https://www.citigroup.com/global/news/perspective/2025/remarks-ceo-jane-fraser-citi-2025-annual-stockholders-meeting.
19. Matt Sigelman, Joseph Fuller, and Alex Martin, *Skills-Based Hiring: The Long Road from Pronouncements to Practice*, Feb. 2024, Burning Glass Institute, https://www.burningglassinstitute.org/research/skills-based-hiring-2024.
20. Byron Auguste, 'In this video, I share the story of my family's path into the American middle class,' LinkedIn, 2025, https://www.linkedin.com/posts/byronauguste_in-

this-video-i-share-the-story-of-my-family-activity-7343778245877637120-Sxi_/.

21. Janet Bush and Michael Chui, hosts, *Forward Thinking*, podcast, 'Forward Thinking on Making Labor Markets Work Smarter – for People and Companies – with Beth Cobert and Byron Auguste,' McKinsey Global Institute, Nov. 17, 2021, https://www.mckinsey.com/featured-insights/future-of-work/forward-thinking-on-making-labor-markets-work-smarter-for-people-and-companies-with-beth-cobert-and-byron-auguste.

22. Byron Auguste, email message to Aneesh Raman, Aug. 15, 2024.

23. Nickle LaMoreaux, 'AI Skills & Performance,' video, LinkedIn, July 2025, https://www.linkedin.com/posts/nickle-lamoreaux_ai-skills-performance-activity-7351619254950985731-2vYW/.

24. Sridhar Pappu, 'That Championship Season,' *UCLA Magazine*, Oct. 7, 2024, https://newsroom.ucla.edu/magazine/basketball-john-wooden-10th-ncaa-championship-oral-history.

25. 'The Wizard's Wisdom: "Woodenisms,"' ESPN.com, June 4, 2010, https://www.espn.com/mens-college-basketball/news/story?id=5249709.

26. Markus Brinsa, 'Gen Z vs. the AI Office – Who Broke Work, and Who's Actually Drowning?,' LinkedIn, Sept. 2, 2025, https://www.linkedin.com/pulse/gen-z-vs-ai-office-who-broke-work-whos-actually-drowning-brinsa-zni1c/.

27. Isabel Berwick, 'Want Happy Staff? Coach Them,' *Financial Times*, Oct. 23, 2024, https://www.ft.com/content/3ae8534f-1aff-4142-bf1d-dff1d91c02c7.

28. Teuila Hanson and Aneesh Raman, 'How to Create Leaders Who Coach, Rather Than Command,' *Fast Company*, April 28, 2025, https://www.fastcompany.com/91323164/how-to-create-leaders-who-coach-rather-than-command.
29. Eric Van Nostrand, 'Small Business and Entrepreneurship in the Post-COVID Expansion,' U.S. Department of the Treasury, Sept. 3, 2024, https://home.treasury.gov/news/featured-stories/small-business-and-entrepreneurship-in-the-post-covid-expansion.
30. 'Micro-, Small and Medium-sized Enterprises Day,' United Nations, accessed Nov. 23, 2025, https://www.un.org/en/observances/micro-small-medium-businesses-day.
31. 'Establishment Age and Survival Data,' Business Employment Dynamics, U.S. Bureau of Labor Statistics, last modified Oct. 30, 2024, https://www.bls.gov/bdm/bdmage.htm.
32. 'A Digital Representation of the Global Economy,' LinkedIn Economic Graph, accessed Nov. 17, 2025, https://economicgraph.linkedin.com/.
33. LinkedIn Talent Solutions, 'Conversations with CHROs: Aneesh Raman of LinkedIn with CTO Séverine Charbon at Publicis Groupe,' YouTube, May 27, 2025, www.youtube.com/watch?v=1nG_a47l-jY.

Chapter 8: Economies Need Innovation from All, for All

1. Kate Kallot, interview for book, Sept. 19, 2025.
2. Ministry of Information, Communications, and Digital Economy, Kenya, 'Kenya National AI Strategy,' Global Partnership for Sustainable Development, March 30, 2025, www.data4sdgs.org/resources/kenya-national-ai-strategy.

Notes

3. World Bank Group, *An Evaluation of the World Bank Group's Support to Electricity Access in Sub-Saharan Africa, 2015–24*.
4. John H. Cochrane, 'A Misunderstood Decade,' *Coolidge Review*, Winter 2024, https://coolidgefoundation.org/blog/a-misunderstood-decade/.
5. David E. Nye, *Electrifying America: Social Meanings of a New Technology, 1880–1940* (Cambridge, MA: MIT Press, 1990).
6. Maria Flynn, interview for book, Aug. 19, 2025.
7. Michael Frith, 'Sprawling Biopolis Jazzes Up Singapore's Science Scene,' *Nature Medicine* 9, no. 12 (2003): 1440, https://doi.org/10.1038/nm1203-1440a.
8. Sharanjit Leyl, 'Singapore Grows Biomedical Industry in a Decade,' video, *BBC News*, Nov. 5, 2013, https://www.bbc.com/news/av/business-24799516.
9. 'What We Do,' Tennessee STEM Innovation Network, accessed Nov. 24, 2025, https://www.tsin.org/what-we-do/.
10. 'Innovation Hub at Research Park,' Research & Innovation, Texas Tech University, accessed Nov. 24, 2025, https://www.depts.ttu.edu/research/research-park/.
11. 'P-TECH Schools: A Win for Colorado Students,' Colorado Succeeds, Aug. 5, 2016, accessed Nov. 24, 2025, https://coloradosucceeds.org/resource/p-tech-schools-win-colorado-students/.
12. Christopher Doyle, 'Pennsylvania Colleges Launch Tech Workforce Consortium,' GovTech, June 17, 2025, https://www.govtech.com/education/higher-ed/pennsylvania-colleges-launch-tech-workforce-consortium.

13. Paul Cheek, interview for book, Sept. 23, 2024.
14. 'AI Skills Passport,' EY, accessed Nov. 23, 2025, https://www.ey.com/en_gl/ai-skills-passport.
15. Billy Perrigo, 'The Workers Behind AI Rarely See Its Rewards – This Indian Startup Wants to Fix That,' *Time*, July 27, 2023, https://time.com/6297403/the-workers-behind-ai-rarely-see-its-rewards-this-indian-startup-wants-to-fix-that/.
16. Vivek Seshadri, interview for book, July 1, 2025.
17. Silvia Lara, 'Skills-Based Hiring: Increasing Access to Opportunity,' LinkedIn Economic Graph Research Institute, March 3, 2025, https://economicgraph.linkedin.com/content/dam/me/economicgraph/en-us/PDF/skills-based-hiring-march-2025.pdf.
18. European Commission, *The Future of European Competitiveness: In-Depth Analysis and Recommendations (Part B)* (Brussels: European Commission, 2024), 270, https://commission.europa.eu/document/download/ec1409c1-d4b4-4882-8bdd-3519f86bbb92_en?filename=The%20future%20of%20European%20competitiveness_%20In-depth%20analysis%20and%20recommendations_0.pdf.
19. 'Executive Order Emphasizes Skills over Degrees for Federal Jobs,' Society for Human Resource Management, July 1, 2020, https://www.shrm.org/topics-tools/news/talent-acquisition/executive-order-emphasizes-skills-degrees-federal-jobs.
20. Andrew Smalley, 'States Consider Elimination of Degree Requirements,' The National Conference of State Legislatures (NCSL), Oct. 4, 2023, https://www.ncsl.

Notes

org/education/states-consider-elimination-of-degree-requirements.

21. 'News Release: Gov. Cox Launches Skills-First Hiring Initiative for State Government,' Governor of Utah Official Website, Dec. 13, 2022, https://governor.utah.gov/press/news-release-gov-cox-launches-skills-first-hiring-initiative-for-state-government/.

22. 'Empowering Progress: Harnessing Skills-Based Strategies to Drive Public Sector Excellence,' National Governors Association, Feb. 6, 2025, https://www.nga.org/publications/empowering-progress-harnessing-skills-based-strategies-to-drive-public-sector-excellence/.

23. Maria Anguiano, interview for book, Aug. 4, 2025.

24. 'LE Annual Report,' Arizona State University Learning, last modified Dec. 20, 2024, https://learning.asu.edu/wp-content/uploads/2024/12/LE_Annual-Report-Oct24_v1_20Dec24_Interactive.pdf.

25. 'About WGU,' Western Governors University, accessed Nov. 24, 2025, https://www.wgu.edu/about.html.

26. 'Empowering the Workforce in the Context of a Skills-First Approach,' OECD, June 24, 2025, www.oecd.org/en/publications/empowering-the-workforce-in-the-context-of-a-skills-first-approach_345b6528-en/full-report/skills-first-in-oecd-countries-concepts-trends-and-implications-for-the-labour-market_0d6ba66f.html.

27. Jordan Novet, 'Microsoft Expects to Spend $80 Billion on AI-Enabled Data Centers in Fiscal 2025,' CNBC, Jan. 3, 2025, https://www.cnbc.com/2025/01/03/microsoft-expects-to-spend-80-billion-on-ai-data-centers-in-fy-2025.

html; Dale Denwalt, 'Google Announces Major Investment in Oklahoma: Here's How Much, Where,' *The Oklahoman*, Aug. 13, 2025, https://www.oklahoman.com/story/business/2025/08/13/google-announces-new-data-center-in-stillwater-expansion-in-pryor/85640825007/; 'Amazon Plans to Invest $20 Billion in Pennsylvania to Expand Cloud Computing Infrastructure and Advance AI Innovation,' About Amazon, June 9, 2025, https://www.aboutamazon.com/news/aws/amazon-pennsylvania-investment-cloud-infrastructure-ai-innovation; Tae Kim, 'AI Infrastructure Drives $750 Billion in Data Center Investment,' *Barron's*, July 8, 2025. https://www.barrons.com/articles/ai-data-centers-nvidia-openai-adbe1545.

28. Natasha Singer, 'Microsoft Pledges $4 Billion Toward A.I. Education,' *New York Times*, July 9, 2025, https://www.nytimes.com/2025/07/09/business/microsoft-ai-education.html.

29. American Federation of Teachers, 'AFT to Launch National Academy for AI Instruction with Microsoft, OpenAI, Anthropic and United Federation of Teachers,' news release, July 8, 2025, https://www.aft.org/press-release/aft-launch-national-academy-ai-instruction-microsoft-openai-anthropic-and-united.

30. 'AFT to Launch National Academy for AI Instruction with Microsoft, OpenAI, Anthropic and United Federation of Teachers.'

31. Melanie Boyer, 'Teachers at the Helm: New National AI Academy Prioritizes Educators in Classroom Tech,' American Federation of Teachers, July 11, 2025, https://

Notes

www.aft.org/news/teachers-helm-new-national-ai-academy-prioritizes-educators-classroom-tech.

Chapter 9: Nobody Beats You at Being You

1. Chris Williamson, '44 Harsh Truths About The Game Of Life – Naval Ravikant (4K),' posted March 31, 2025, YouTube, https://www.youtube.com/watch?v=KyfUysrNaco.
2. Nilofer Merchant, 'The First Step to Being Powerful,' *Harvard Business Review*, Nov. 8, 2013, https://hbr.org/2013/11/the-first-step-to-being-powerful; Nilofer Merchant, *11 Rules for Creating Value in the #SocialEra* (Boston: Harvard Business Review Press, 2012); Nilofer Merchant, *The Power of Onlyness: Make Your Wild Ideas Mighty Enough to Dent the World* (New York: Viking, 2017).
3. Nilofer Merchant, interview for book, Sept. 16, 2025.
4. Merchant, *The Power of Onlyness*, 8.
5. Merchant, *The Power of Onlyness*, 8.
6. Ryan Roslansky, host, *The Path*, podcast, season 1, episode 3, 'From Doorman to Boardroom: CEO John Henry on How to Leverage Your "Onlyness,"' LinkedIn.com, Aug. 22, 2023, https://www.linkedin.com/pulse/from-doorman-boardroom-ceo-john-henry-how-leverage-your-roslansky/.
7. Ryan Roslansky, host, *The Path*, podcast, season 3, episode 5, '"I Broke Every Norm": Leena Nair's Path to CHANEL CEO,' LinkedIn.com, April 29, 2025, https://www.linkedin.com/pulse/i-broke-every-norm-leena-nairs-path-chanel-ceo-ryan-roslansky-shnpc.
8. Ryan Roslansky, host, *The Path*, podcast, season 3, episode 6, '"Anyone Who Tells You to Follow Your Passion Is

Already Rich." How Scott Galloway Paved His Path,' LinkedIn.com, June 3, 2025, https://www.linkedin.com/pulse/anyone-who-tells-you-follow-your-passion-already-rich-ryan-roslansky-tdgtc/.

9. Ryan Rolansky, host, *The Path*, podcast, season 2, episode 5, '"You Really Have to Stand Up for Yourself. You Gotta Get Back Up." How Barbara Corcoran Used Insults as Motivation to Boost Her Career,' LinkedIn.com, March 14, 2024, https://www.linkedin.com/pulse/you-really-have-stand-up-yourself-gotta-get-back-how-used-roslansky-7zsvf/.

10. Taylor Locke, 'Why Barbara Corcoran "Felt Like an Absolute Fraud" After Selling Her Business for $66 Million,' CNBC, Feb. 27, 2020, https://www.cnbc.com/2020/02/27/why-barbara-corcoran-felt-like-a-fraud-after-selling-her-business.html.

11. Merchant, interview for book.

12. Apollo 13: *Survival*, directed by Peter Middleton (Insight Film, 2024), Netflix.

Chapter 10: Open to Work

1. 'Networks, Not AI or Search, Are the #1 Trusted Source Amid Information Overload, LinkedIn Research Finds,' LinkedIn Newsroom, Aug. 26, 2025, https://news.linkedin.com/2025/networks--not-ai-or-search--are-the--1-trusted-source-amid-infor.

About the Authors

RYAN ROSLANSKY is the CEO of LinkedIn, the world's largest and most powerful network of professionals, and executive vice president of Microsoft Office and Copilot. Ryan previously held the role of global head of product at LinkedIn, where he oversaw all teams responsible for building and creating the next generation of LinkedIn products and experiences. He is also the host of *The Path*, the video series, podcast, and newsletter about careers and work. Through these roles, Ryan is shaping where work goes next to create greater economic opportunity for the global workforce.

ANEESH RAMAN is the chief economic opportunity officer of LinkedIn, where he works with leaders across societies and sectors to shape the global response to the historic changes hitting work. Previously, he served as senior adviser on economic strategy and public affairs to the State of California, led economic impact at Facebook, worked as a presidential speechwriter, and was a war correspondent. A graduate of

OPEN TO WORK

Harvard College and a former Fulbright Scholar, he serves on the boards of the College Futures Foundation and Shanti Bhavan Children's Project.